THE HEART OF
TIBETAN BUDDHISM

THE HEART
OF TIBETAN
BUDDHISM

Advice for Life, Death,
and Enlightenment

KHENPO SHERAB SANGPO

SHAMBHALA

Shambhala Publications, Inc.
2129 13th Street
Boulder, Colorado 80302
www.shambhala.com

Cover art: Courtesy of Robert Beer
Cover design: Daniel Urban-Brown
Interior design: Katrina Noble

9 8 7 6 5 4 3 2 1
First Edition
Printed in the United States of America

Shambhala Publications makes every effort to print on acid-free, recycled paper.
Shambhala Publications is distributed worldwide by Penguin Random House, Inc., and its subsidiaries.

LIBRARY OF CONGRESS CATALOGING-IN-PUBLICATION DATA
Names: Sangpo, Khenpo Sherab, author.
Title: The heart of Tibetan Buddhism: advice for life, death, and
    enlightenment / Khenpo Sherab Sangpo.
Description: Boulder, Colorado: Shambhala, [2024]
Identifiers: LCCN 2023027925 | ISBN 9781645472063 (trade paperback)
    Subjects: LCSH: Rnying-ma-pa (Sect)—Doctrines. | Spiritual life—
    Buddhism. | Enlightenment (Buddhism)
Classification: LCC BQ7662.4 .S244 2024 | DDC 294.3/444—
    dc23/eng/20230712
LC record available at https://lccn.loc.gov/2023027925

CONTENTS

NOTE ON TRANSLATION

All English translations of verses contained in this book were translated by the author based on lineage teachings he received and a variety of Tibetan-language texts.

HOMAGE TO THE GURU

To respect and prostrate to our gurus is very important, as there is not a single buddha or bodhisattva in the past, present, or future who has achieved or will achieve enlightenment without relying on a spiritual teacher. The *Condensed Perfection of Wisdom Sutra* states,

> Excellent students who have respect for the guru should always rely on qualified gurus. Why is that so? It is from them that the qualities of wisdom arise.

The great eleventh-century Buddhist master Atisha Dipamkara Shrijnana said that until you attain enlightenment, you need a teacher. Therefore, we should do our best to follow a genuine spiritual teacher. All happiness is a result of our teacher's blessing, so we should always remember their kindness. We should recognize our gurus as the source of all supreme qualities. For this reason, I pay homage to my root teachers at the beginning of this book.

The Buddha—the lion of the Shakyas, the great friend of all living creatures, and the fourth Buddha of our fortunate age—gave unbiased teachings suited to the capacities of all beings out of his great compassion and using his skillful means. Cherished by those who wish to obtain liberation from suffering, his sacred Dharma is the source of every temporary and ultimate benefit and happiness.

There are many teachers in whom people have sought temporary and ultimate refuge. Many different spiritual traditions have spread in the world and continue to do so. All have arisen dependent upon the needs of various people. As there is great purpose and benefit in all spiritual traditions, we should respect them, maintain a pure view, and recognize that there is no need for religious hatred. Among these traditions, Buddhism has endured for a very long time, having arisen in India approximately 2,500 years ago.

If we investigate spiritual traditions and, in particular, the scriptures taught by Buddha Shakyamuni, we will understand that he articulated many uniquely valid philosophical views that did not exist in our world prior to his teachings.

The unique essence of the Buddha's teachings is his understanding of dependent origination. This view and practice are exclusive to Buddhism; the Buddhist scriptures are indispensable for understanding them. The more I examine this spiritual path, the more I appreciate how vast and profound it is, as it never expounds logic for no reason.

Whoever we are, we should reflect upon these subjects with an open mind so that we can serve society to the best of our ability. The responsibility falls on the shoulders of us all—great and small—to examine our spiritual life and to carefully consider our responsibilities to other living beings with whom we share this world.

My Root Teachers

Khenchen Padma Tsewang

In 1979, when I was eight, I met my first root teacher, Khenchen Padma Tsewang, who was recognized as the reincarnation of the great master Ngawang Chöpal Gyatso (Lochen Dharmashri), the brother of Rigdzin Terdak Lingpa. As my parents were nomadic, I lived with my

Khenpo Sherab Sangpo's root teachers. *From left to right*: Adzom Drukpa Thupten Padma Trinle, Khenchen Padma Tsewang, Khenchen Chöying Chapdal, Khenchen Jigme Phuntsok, and Khangsar Tenpe Wangchuk. Pencil drawing by Bao Nguyen.

grandparents in the village of Arikza in Kham, in southeastern Tibet. My grandparents knew Khenchen Padma Tsewang and decided to send me to this great master to learn grammar and how to write the Tibetan alphabet.

In 1986, Khenchen Padma Tsewang opened the monastic university Ngetön Shedrup Targyé Ling, at Ngagyur Nyingma Gyalwa Pukang, the monastery where I began studying Buddhist philosophy and practicing meditation. During this time, we formed a very close teacher-student relationship that lasted over fifteen years. I wrote down his oral teachings, served as his personal attendant, and traveled with him when he was invited to teach at other monasteries.

Throughout his life, he demonstrated his great capacities through his compassionate conduct and profound knowledge. I stayed with Khenchen Padma Tsewang at his monastery until 1992, when he sent me to receive teachings from Khenchen Jigme Phuntsok, my second root teacher. We parted at that time when I began studying at Sêrta Larung Gar. However, whenever I returned home, I would visit him and he would give me further instructions and advice.

When it came time for us to part for the last time, Khenchen Padma Tsewang told me to teach with a good motivation as this would be how I would most benefit others. Later, toward the end of his life in 2000, he sent me to teach at Ka-Nying Shedrup Ling, a monastery at Boudhanath in Kathmandu, Nepal. He told me that after I was done teaching there I could go wherever I wished and do whatever I thought was best. He passed away two years later in 2002 while I was teaching in Nepal.

Khenchen Jigme Phuntsok

In 1980, Khenchen Jigme Phuntsok, my second root teacher, opened the monastic university Sêrta Larung Gar, where I studied Buddhist philosophy and received teachings on mind training, along with empowerments, Dzogchen teachings, and special oral instructions given directly by Khenchen Jigme Phuntsok. I studied there for six years, from 1992 to 1995, and again from 1997 to 2000.

In 1999 I received Dzogchen teachings on Patrul Rinpoche's commentary on *Striking the Vital Point in Three Statements*, the famous three lines spoken by the early Dzogchen master Garab Dorje as his last testament to his disciple Manjushrimitra.

To create a conducive environment for receiving these special teachings, Khenchen Jigme Phuntsok had us climb two hours to the top of a nearby mountain where he gave us oral instructions for two weeks. During this time I told one of my Dharma friends that we would never forget our guru's great kindness and the way that he had given us those Dzogchen teachings.

On the second day, Khenchen Jigme Phuntsok said, "I am going to introduce you to the nature of your mind." After we had chanted supplication prayers to the Dzogchen lineage, while resting his wisdom mind in the absolute nature of the dharmakaya, he suddenly introduced us to the nature of mind using various instructions. At the end, he asked us three times, "What is mind?" and paused without speaking. He said that what had happened in that moment was that our past thoughts had ceased, our future thoughts had not yet arisen, and that in between, our awareness was free from all clinging. He told us that we should recognize what is spontaneously present, beyond grasping. However, without devotion, that would not be possible as recognition arises only when devotion to the lineage is present. In that way, he spontaneously and effortlessly introduced us to the nature of mind.

The most memorable time of my life was when I received those amazing Dzogchen teachings from Khenchen Jigme Phuntsok. In 2004, in the final moments before his passing, his heart advice was "Do not lose your own path, do not disturb others' minds."

Khenchen Chöying Chapdal

In 1995, I spent one year studying with Khenchen Chöying Chapdal, a recognized reincarnation of Rongzom Chökyi Zangpo (Rongzompa), a great Nyingma master of the eleventh century. In 1979, he started teaching Buddhist philosophy at Sêrta Ludo in Golok in eastern Tibet.

Khenchen Chöying Chapdal lived an austere and humble life despite his fame as a great teacher. One of his most noble qualities was that he had completely diminished his attachment and grasping at self by practicing genuine renunciation. Therefore, he was known as the second Milarepa in Tibet at that time. Once, when Khenchen Padma Tsewang taught us *The Words of My Perfect Teacher*, he said that there had been many great masters in Tibet. Yet of them all, the one who was a genuine Dharma practitioner was Khenchen Chöying Chapdal—therefore, we should pray for his long life.

Khenchen Chöying Chapdal had the most important instructions on the commentary of the *prajnaparamita* written by his root teacher, the great Nyingma master Bötrul Dongak Tenpe Nyima. I was fortunate to receive that commentary, along with Longchenpa's commentary on the *Guhyagarbha Tantra* and other precious teachings, directly from him.

Each day before he would give teachings, Khenchen Chöying Chapdal would offer food to his students. We would sit and eat together, listening to him as he talked about his teachers—how he had found them—and about Tibetan culture during his lifetime. Everyone enjoyed this time together and followed his example by sharing our food and tea with one another when we gathered for meals.

Khenchen Chöying Chapdal showed great dedication to the Dharma by teaching until the day he passed away. He told his students that his death was approaching and asked them to prepare a three-day celebration to bring happiness to everyone. On the third day, after lunch, he peacefully passed away at the age of seventy-seven. I was deeply moved and inspired by my third root teacher's simple life of renunciation.

Adzom Drukpa Thupten Padma Trinle

Khenchen Padma Tsewang also sent me to study with my fourth root teacher. In 1996, I went to Adzom Gar monastery in the Tromtar region of Kham in eastern Tibet to receive experiential instructions called *nyong-tri*, from Adzom Drukpa Thupten Padma Trinle.

When I arrived at his monastery, I presented a letter of introduction written to him by my first root teacher. The letter said that I was a good student; it listed my qualifications and requested that he give me pointing-out instructions.

Usually when students studied with Adzom Drukpa Rinpoche, they would have to first complete the preliminaries. However, because of the letter of introduction, I was able to skip ahead in his curriculum to practice *shamatha* meditation.

Adzom Drukpa Rinpoche gave me instructions and then I would meditate on them for a designated period of time. Then he would give me the next set of instructions, and so forth, as I progressed. I received all the special oral instructions of the Dzogchen Nyingtik lineage from him.

While there, I had the sincere wish to leave everything behind and to meditate alone for the rest of my life. I went to see Adzom Drukpa Rinpoche at his hermitage and offered him a silk ceremonial scarf (*khata*), an image of a stupa and one of the Buddha, and some money. Adzom Drukpa Rinpoche accepted everything that I offered except the money. When I began prostrating before him, he told me immediately that I had the wrong plan for my life. I had not said anything to him, but I knew that my fourth root teacher was commenting on my wish to abandon everything to meditate.

Adzom Drukpa Rinpoche asked me how many years I had been studying Buddhist philosophy, and he told me that I should use my knowledge to teach in order to benefit others. He gave me permission to teach Dzogchen, and I promised that I would. I asked for his advice on what to do if I encountered obstacles. He told me that after I had practiced 1,500,000 Vajrakilaya mantra recitations, I would have no obstacles.

Because of Khenchen Padma Tsewang's letter of introduction, Adzom Drukpa Rinpoche loved and trusted me. He often gave empowerments secretly, but he would send other students to find me so that I could receive those empowerments. I received six months of Dzogchen teachings and other empowerments at his peaceful monastery.

I wanted to remain there, as it was conducive to meditation; however, he told me that I had received everything from him. Therefore, there was no need to stay longer. After parting at that time, I was fortunate to have the opportunity to meet with Adzom Drukpa Rinpoche three more times before he passed away in 2001.

Khangsar Tenpe Wangchuk

I met Khangsar Tenpe Wangchuk in 2012, during a monthlong Dzogchen teaching that he gave at his monastery, Akyong Khangsar in

Golok in eastern Tibet. Initially I was hesitant to attend his teachings because I felt no connection to him and thought that I had received enough prior teachings. However, one of my cousins assured me that his teachings would be unique and different from what I had received before. Therefore, I decided to attend.

Moved by the power of his wondrous Dzogchen teachings, I requested the pointing-out instructions from him. Although three thousand students were attending his teachings, Khangsar Tenpe Wangchuk gave the pointing-out instructions to only ten students at a time. In my group, three had never received these instructions and seven had heard them from other teachers. Khangsar Tenpe Wangchuk's pointing-out instructions were very special and spontaneous. During that time, I was powerfully hit by each word.

On the last day of the teachings, I asked him to give me a recording of his Dzogchen teachings so that I could listen to them in the future. He said that if I promised to teach Jigme Lingpa's *Yeshe Lama*, a crucial Dzogchen text, that he would give the recording to me. I accepted immediately.

In addition, he told me that he had practiced ten different preliminary practice texts. However, he had recognized the nature of mind through the blessings of *The Chariot of Liberation*, a treasure text revealed by Dudjom Lingpa. Then he gave me the reading transmission, encouraged me to practice this profound preliminary practice, and advised me to give it to my students. In 2014, in accordance with Khangsar Tenpe Wangchuk's wishes, many of my students started practicing this ritual text.

Khangsar Tenpe Wangchuk passed away in 2014, and his final words of advice to his disciples were:

Compassion for sentient beings, respect for cause and effect, devotion to the Three Jewels, taking to heart the pith instructions, love for Dharma friends and for the ordained sangha in particular—let there be harmony, perfect observance of the vows, and service to the teachings. Please, never forget this advice.

PREFACE

There are hundreds of Buddhist scriptures and innumerable sacred commentaries written by the Buddha's wise, discerning followers that are widely available. For authentic aspirants who wish to attain liberation, there is certainly no scarcity of teachings and no great need for the simple words that I have written here.

Still, to sustain the invaluable, precious teachings of the Buddha and to prevent them from declining—and because I entered the Buddhist path at an early age, continued to receive teachings on the sutras and tantras from many kind spiritual teachers, and have spent my whole life studying them—I would like to introduce the inner meaning of Buddhism according to my experience.

In this short book I explain the essence of the teachings in ordinary language to help practitioners who, from the stillness of meditation, would like to realize the nature of their own mind.

Here are the oral instructions passed down from generations of holy masters that I have taken to heart, practiced, and appreciated deeply through my experience—indeed, these precious instructions have guided and continue to guide my life.

With utmost faith in the Mahayana path, I encourage you to practice the precious mind of bodhichitta, the kind mind possessing the altruistic aspiration to enlightenment, as it is the unmistaken cause of genuine happiness and therefore indispensable for everyone. If we practice this profound essence of the Buddhadharma, we can transform ourselves completely through its amazing qualities.

Therefore, I am happy to have written this concise guide for practicing bodhichitta. If you have time, please study it closely, meditate on its teachings, and integrate the resulting wisdom into your daily life.

PART ONE

Entering the Path of Practice

When we enter the great door of the Dharma, it is important to understand the preciousness of the teachings and to have an aspiration to practice them. By carefully investigating the teachings, we gain conviction in our path and certainty in the value of the spiritual teachings that inspire us to practice correctly.

Developing faith in Buddhism for no reason—having no idea of its essential meaning, direction, or path—or in dependence on mistaken or incorrect reasons is blind faith. This was not recommended by the Buddha or other great spiritual masters—such as Longchenpa, Mipham Rinpoche, and Patrul Rinpoche—in our Nyingma tradition, the earliest tradition in Tibetan Buddhism. Therefore, it is important to develop what is called confident faith by investigating the validity of the teachings with your own intelligence and wisdom. As the great yogin Milarepa says,

Insightful wisdom, compassion, and character—these three are continuous guides on the path.

These days, some people would use Buddha Shakyamuni's teachings as a tool to accomplish mundane purposes: to feed themselves, to build their wealth and reputation, or just for temporary good fortune. Some claim to be able to accomplish worldly aims using the Buddha's power; however, if the desired aims are not accomplished, it brings disparagement and destruction to the teachings by causing them to be avoided or discounted. Quite a few people accumulate the karma of abandoning the Dharma by rebelling against it or by developing deeply distorted views about it. The cause of this is following a spiritual path out of blind faith without first investigating its principles and coming to know the inner meaning of the Dharma.

Therefore, before embarking on the path, we must examine the Buddha and his teachings with the three pure analyses: direct perception, logical inference, and scriptural inference. Once we have attained faith through knowledge, we can practice the Dharma throughout our lives. In the *Shrimahabalatantrarajasutra*, the Buddha advises,

> Just as gold is tested by being burned, cut, and rubbed,
> the wise should accept my words only after examining them,
> not merely out of faith or other such reasons.

The Buddha clearly advised his followers not to practice his teachings solely out of respect, for no particular reason, or because of their renown. The process of investigating the teachings has been the traditional way from ancient times to the present, and this is one characteristic that distinguishes the Buddha's sublime teachings from other paths. Therefore, we should not rely upon the personality of a teacher but upon the validity of the teachings.

By examining the teachings repeatedly, a practitioner comes to understand what is to be practiced and what is to be abandoned, and he or she should practice accordingly. This is the unexcelled way of entering the Buddha's sacred teachings. The Buddha taught the four reliances shortly before his passing:

> Rely on the message of the teacher, not on his personality;
> rely on the meaning, not just on the words;
> rely on the real meaning, not on the provisional one;
> rely on your wisdom mind, not on your ordinary judgmental
>   mind.

In ancient India, for example, the scholar Udbhatasiddhasvamin was extremely learned in the Brahmanic scriptures. He analyzed and examined the Buddha's teachings thoroughly, and once he understood the logic behind them, he developed faith based on reason. In the *Vishesastava*, the verses of praise to the Buddha at the beginning of the Kangyur, part of the Tibetan Buddhist canon, he states,

> I have no loyalty to the Buddha,
> nor do I have hatred for followers of Kapila.
> Whatever is based on logic—
> that is an authentic teacher and spiritual path.

Only after we have examined the teachings objectively and understood them clearly should we enter the Buddhist spiritual path. Being forced to become a Buddhist—without being interested in or without prior knowledge of the teachings—is not an authentic way of entering the door of the Dharma.

The Buddha advises us not to explain the teachings to those without interest, respect, or faith. People should never be forced to become a Buddhist against their wishes. However, if someone has a genuine interest and wishes to become a Buddhist due to a proper understanding of the meaningfulness of the teachings, it is permissible for any being to enter the practice of the Buddha's teachings. It is a spiritual path open to all.

When the Buddha taught the Vinaya—one of the three collections of the Buddhist scriptures, devoted to monastic discipline—many people in India developed faith and took ordination. According to one story, some fishermen who lived where the Buddha was teaching regretted the harm that they had done while fishing. They were dejected because they thought that people with the karma of killing and with their inferior status in society would not be allowed to join the disciples (*shravakas*) as monks who practiced the Buddha's teachings.

Shariputra, one of the Buddha's foremost disciples, asked them why they were so sad and unhappy. They replied that they wanted to become monastics but were unsuitable due to their low-caste profession. Shariputra replied,

> In these teachings of the Buddha, caste is not important, bloodline is not important! Practice is of most importance! If you take ordination from the Buddha and cast off your negative karma through practice, why would you be unsuitable?

The fishermen became monks and entered the door of the Dharma. No matter who you are, you have an equal capacity for attainment and the right to follow the Buddhist path. It is a spiritual path that does no harm to others and that benefits all. As Gendun Chöphel writes,

> The teachings from the founder of Buddhism, Buddha Shakyamuni, and other qualified masters have given people in the various countries where it has spread vast control of their own minds; it purifies their mind, transforming them.

Various Personalities and Paths

Some people have no belief in the Dharma or in future lives and crave the happiness of this life alone. They try to subdue their enemies and protect their friends, passing their lives aspiring only to that.

Other people want the happiness of this and future lives, and they strive in their worldly endeavors and in their practice of the Dharma to obtain these.

Others understand that the happiness of this and future lives is only temporary and not ultimate, with no essence at all; they strive solely for what transcends it—the ultimate, unexcelled state of buddhahood.

Because the Buddha had great skill and wisdom, he taught his students through many vehicles, or systems of thought and practice, such as the Hinayana, Mahayana, Sutrayana, and Tantrayana. Due to the needs of people with different personalities, faculties, and aspirations, he taught various vehicles to set them on the appropriate paths toward temporary and ultimate happiness.

The purpose of these various paths is to help us be good, kindhearted people. If we practice the Dharma well, it protects us from suffering. However, if we do not practice as the Buddha taught, the results will not be attained. As Buddha Shakyamuni points out in the *Gandavyuhasutra*,

> Noble one, think of yourself as someone who is sick,
> of the Dharma as the remedy,
> of your spiritual teacher as a skillful doctor,
> and of diligent practice as the way to recovery.

and,

> I have shown you the path to liberation,
> however, be aware that liberation depends upon yourself.

Everything depends upon whether we practice as the Buddha taught. If we don't, it won't help us. The sun illuminates the world, but those blind since birth do not see what is illuminated by the sun. The Buddha illuminated the world with the sacred Dharma, but it will not help those who are blinded by ignorance. By practicing the path of the Dharma that benefits our mind, if we can sustain it throughout our lives—no matter what happens to us in good or bad situations with our finances, health, or environment—we can be happy and easily deal with our circumstances. Due to our practice, we can maintain a broad perspective and vast aspirations. For instance, some of my friends were very depressed, hot-tempered people with many desires. After practicing the Dharma, they have become happier and less greedy.

If we diligently practice the Buddhadharma, it can powerfully transform us. Authentic practice of the Dharma results in having more peace and freedom, and that is the root of all happiness. As the Buddha says, the happiness of beings can only come from training the mind in noble and ethical attitudes, such as love and compassion. No matter how much outer wealth and property we have, it will not help our inner mental happiness, and often it harms us. Our desires and arrogant ambitions increase all sorts of inner and outer sufferings and bring great harm to our society. All of this happens due to our uncontrolled minds, which lack love, compassion, peace, and happiness.

When we reflect upon it, our current times are extremely volatile and lacking in happiness. Those who cheat others and destroy society appear to multiply daily, harming others with greed and deceit. When peace and happiness are missing, it is a big mistake if we try to create mental and physical happiness only by relying on external material things and do not develop our minds internally. Therefore, it is very important not to fall to the two extremes of either excessive material desires or excessive asceticism; we must abandon both of these in our lives. If we strive to accumulate great wealth out of desire, we harm others and increase our own suffering and delusions. As Mahatma Gandhi suggests,

> If each person kept no more than they needed, this world would be free of poverty and no one would die of hunger or thirst.

Conversely, we cannot accomplish any worldly or spiritual goals with the other extreme of asceticism. In general, poor food, inadequate clothing, and other intense hardships obstruct our health and endanger our life, so they should not be deliberately pursued. Whereas any form of livelihood pursued with honesty, respect, and good conduct is without fault. The Buddha did not say that it is impermissible to seek wealth and enjoyment. Indeed, the Buddha and his followers went to benefactors daily to request food and other donations. Generally speaking, true practitioners of the Dharma have little desire, being content with what they have. Possessing a vastly altruistic motivation as their ultimate intention, true followers of the Buddha have few self-centered goals or activities, as they focus on performing activities for the sake of others. To summarize:

> If we analyze with objective awareness, truth and falsity are
>   distinguished.
> If we understand this spiritual path, it compels belief.
> Therefore, check well; distancing yourself
> from crooked attitudes, enter a straight path!

The Meaning of Dharma

What do we mean by the Dharma? These are the teachings taught by the fully enlightened Buddha that are enjoyed and practiced by spiritually noble beings. It is the path taken by all the buddhas, who perfectly train sentient beings via their teachings. It is the excellent unmistaken advice given by these realized beings.

Most people think that the Dharma is a spiritual tradition of making offerings and saying prayers in monasteries, making requests and saying dedication prayers on behalf of the deceased, conferring empowerments, doing recitations, turning prayer wheels, and performing prostrations and circumambulations—this is mistaken. These are only facets of this spiritual path, performed for temporary purposes, not the actual essence of the Dharma. As Jamgön Kongtrul says,

> Building statues, offering butter lamps, prostration, circum-ambulation, and recitation of prayers: such compounded roots of virtue is the Dharma of worldly beings, the *common Dharma*. Although it is amazing and of fathomless bene-fit, this is not what is called the *sacred Dharma*. Striving to learn, contemplate, and meditate, and keeping the three vows without duplicity—striving in such uncompounded roots of virtue is the *uncommon Dharma* of those who have entered the practice of Buddha's teachings.

The teachings of the Buddha do not need to harm your relation-ships with others. Many of my students have the deep wish to be able to practice Buddhism openly, but they worry that their families and friends will be troubled that they have taken refuge vows and are practicing Buddhists. Their worry stems from their parents' or friends' belief that if they practice the Buddhadharma, they will aban-don their social responsibility in this life or will go to the hell realms after they die.

It is possible for us to choose a religion that is different from the spiritual path of our parents and friends; however, this freedom will not come without suffering when people create arguments over religion. I encourage my students to talk with their parents and friends openly about why they choose to practice Buddhism, and I sincerely hope that they will engage in dialogue about their beliefs without causing harm to one another.

Much suffering can be reduced through understanding. Each person must find a spiritual path that works with their personality and the way that their mind works. For me, Buddhism and meditation are best. However, we must understand that many spiritual traditions exist due to the various needs of cultures and people all over the world. We live in a time when we have the chance to learn about many different cultures and religions; therefore, keeping an open mind about the benefits of each spiritual path and practicing religious tolerance are essential.

Understand that the Dharma is nothing other than a method to improve our intentions and conduct—a method to correctly develop all the good qualities of our minds gradually over time. Although there are many different meanings of the Sanskrit word *Dharma*, in this context it means "the truth that protects and transforms the mind." As the Buddha teaches,

> Beings are liberated through being shown the truth of the Dharma.

The Buddha, who shows the truth of the Dharma that reveals ultimate reality, is like someone who points out the path when we need to go somewhere. When the Buddha reveals the Dharma to beings who are under the control of their own ignorance and confusion, they are protected from the delusion of their minds. Mistaken ideas—such as perceiving what is impermanent to be permanent, suffering to be happiness, and conceiving of an inherent self—are all corrected and transformed by the Dharma into unmistaken authentic spiritual paths. It is the good inner path of a compassionate mind without violence or fear, showing us how to adopt what empowers us and abandon what causes harm, thus freeing us from misfortune and limitations.

If we practice daily, we can gradually recognize the value of the Dharma. The Dharma is not merely intellectual; it is meant to improve our mind. It is important for us to integrate the Dharma into our daily life—otherwise, it will not help our mind. We must mix our mind completely with the Dharma. As Milarepa says,

> It is not enough simply to look at food—you need to eat it.
> It is not enough simply to hear the Dharma—you must
>   meditate.

The Dharma also means the "spiritual path"; that is, the implementation—the actual practice and accomplishment—of the correct method of adopting and abandoning. The gateway to this unmistaken liberating path is to study the Dharma by listening, contemplating, and meditating on it; and by continually investigating, with our own discriminating wisdom, the instructions for practice in the scriptures and their commentaries until we develop a special mental conviction that is free of doubt. Applying everything we learn as a method to subdue our mind transforms our intentions and conduct so that we are kind to one another without ulterior motives and derive joy from helping one another. This is, of course, an essential facet of human life.

All the sutric and tantric teachings of Buddha Shakyamuni's eighty-four thousand collections of teachings are included in the Tripitaka of Vinaya, Sutra Pitaka, and Abhidharma. Together these comprise the Dharma of scriptural transmission and the Dharma of realization that consist of the three higher trainings in morality, concentration, and wisdom. The philosopher Vasubandhu states,

Sacred Buddhadharma has two aspects:
that with a nature of scriptural transmission and that of
realization.
Upholding it is a matter of just teaching it, and practicing it.

And as is taught in the *lamrim* tradition on the stages of the path,

Scriptural Dharma is that which determines or defines how
to practice the Dharma, and the realized Dharma is, once
this has been determined, practicing and accomplishing just
what has been determined; so these two are cause and effect.
For instance, when horses race, they are first shown the track;
then, after they have been shown the track, they race.

Therefore, the spiritual path of the Dharma is a method to abandon
all harmful thoughts, speech, and physical actions. In addition, it is a
method of accomplishing vast benefit for ourselves and others. It is
an excellent union of skillful means and wisdom for beings to attain
happiness and to dispel suffering in the beginning, middle, and final
stages of their development.

The sacred Dharma has three points: (1) by way of conduct and
activity, it is a method to accomplish the temporary and the ultimate
benefit and happiness of living beings; (2) by way of intention and motivation, it is a method to transform all attitudes into love, compassion,
and bodhichitta; and (3) by way of commitment and attainment, it is a
method to improve this and future lives until liberation is attained.

Buddha Shakyamuni's teachings are primarily a method to
subdue the mind. The pure realization of the Buddha's teachings
depends solely upon whether a person's mind is subdued or not; it
does not depend on external things. The Buddha admonishes in the
Pratimokshasutra:

Commit not a single unwholesome action,
cultivate a wealth of virtue,
tame completely the mind—
this is the teaching of the buddhas.

Therefore, if we cannot familiarize ourselves and train in this secret instruction of the mind, we will not be liberated from suffering through austerities of the body or speech alone. It is important for us to understand that the mind itself is the root of all. We must abandon harmful conduct and practice good conduct to achieve temporary and lasting happiness. What does this mean? The great master Nagarjuna said that unwholesome actions are created out of attachment, hatred, and ignorance. Virtuous actions are created out of no attachment, hatred, and ignorance.

Accordingly, it is whether delusion—such as attachment—motivates an act that determines whether the intent and conduct is virtuous or not. Committing acts or causing others to commit acts of body, speech, or mind that harm other living beings is not virtuous. Performing acts or causing others to perform acts of body, speech, and mind that bring benefit to others is virtuous.

Therefore, the root of virtue depends on our intention—on our mind. Whatever we impute with our mind is what appears; appearances do not arise as external objects. In *Speech of Delight*, Mipham Rinpoche's commentary on Shantarakshita's *Ornament of the Middle Way*, he affirms,

> To resolve that *the nature of all phenomena arises from our
> mind itself* is the supreme and exceptional quality of the
> philosophy of Buddhism. This is the way that things appear,
> and for the practice of meditation it is the sacred key point of
> the oral instructions . . . . Like the appearances of last night's
> dream, for example, if other methods are used to try to dispel

those [dreamlike] appearances, there is no end to it, but just understanding that appearances arise from the mind itself makes them dissolve as soon as they appear. We should understand that all of existence is like that.

Therefore, our own mind decides if we will go from life to life harming other beings or if we will turn our ego away from selfishness and toward bodhichitta, offering sentient beings our joy and happiness until we all attain enlightenment. All this depends completely on what we do with our own mind. Each of us is responsible for the well-being and happiness of all beings, including ourselves. As Longchenpa observes,

Although all these appearances are not real,
through clinging to duality, illusory interdependence appears.
Until the sphere of duality subsides,
karmic cause and effect exist as its emanation,
and all karmic formations of mind are produced.
Since they are just appearances to mind—mind's
imputations—
strive to subdue the emanating mind!

Pride, hatred, jealousy, and other delusions arise from the mind. In dependence upon them we act in ways that harm the body, speech, and mind of ourselves and other living beings. This causes unhappiness for ourselves and others; therefore, we suffer. Conversely, if we develop positive mental states of love, compassion, and bodhichitta—training our mind in emptiness, selflessness, and so on—many inconceivable good qualities that exist in our mind will manifest. Through meditation we train in teachings that are beyond the comprehension of ordinary beings. Accordingly, the cause for happiness in this and in future lives—the cause for the attainment of liberation and enlightenment—is the mind. The Buddha says,

Freedom is happiness,
being controlled by others is suffering.
Genuine freedom is happiness of the mind.
That happiness can only come from training the mind and
    attitudes.

If our mind transforms in positive ways, it becomes the root of all success in worldly and spiritual endeavors, a foundation for every temporary and ultimate benefit and joy. If our mind transforms in negative ways, it becomes a primary cause of ruining ourselves and destroying others; and there is no way to liberate ourselves or others from endless suffering. The root that induces all harmful activities is the mind. This is why we must bring our mind under control.

If we do this, we are like a buddha who, by manifesting realized qualities, accomplishes inconceivable deeds. If we bring our mind fully under control, the result is liberation and happiness. If our mind is out of control, the result is the suffering of samsara, the endless cycle of existence. We have been wandering out of control in samsara, accumulating negative karma from beginningless time. So how could we not suffer for it? If we practice the Dharma of not harming others, we can rid ourselves of all negative conduct, and our mind will not be disturbed by unhappiness or discomfort. The Kadampa master Dromtönpa said that if you don't change your mental attitude, then no matter what you do, you will not find peace and happiness of mind.

As Buddhists, we believe that the perfect means of subduing our mind was taught by the Buddha alone. If we seek happiness within the mind, we discover ultimate happiness. If we seek happiness outside the mind, we discover that external prosperity often brings much suffering. Therefore, no matter what Buddhist scripture we study through listening, contemplating, and meditating, it is nothing but a source of methods for taming our uncontrolled mind. In addition, importantly, when we develop love, compassion, and bodhichitta in the mind, we enhance calm-abiding meditation, which gives us a sense of deep peace beyond external conditions. If we have these qualities, no matter where we live, whether we have positive or negative people around us, whether we are rich or poor or experience pleasure or pain, whether we hear praise or blame—whatever happens, we will be happy. Therefore, the great teacher Atisha Dipamkara advises in his *Aims* to

Aim your mind at the Dharma.
Aim your Dharma practice at simple living.

"Aim your mind at the Dharma" means we need a genuine refuge and protection from samsara. You might think that the best protection is your property, money, or belongings. But from the Buddhist point of view, no matter how much you enjoy samsaric pleasure, it cannot give you genuine happiness, as these things are illusory. The Dharma is the best protection because if you practice it properly, it is inevitable that you will obtain the ultimate benefit and happiness of liberation.

"Aim your Dharma practice at simple living" means that if you have a simple life, you will have less worry. If you continually enjoy samsaric pleasure, your desire will never be satisfied. Wanting ever more creates even more obstacles. Reducing the amount of stress and worry in your life through simple living reduces your anger, fear, disappointment, and anxiety. We should practice these two things for our entire life until our death.

In short, the Dharma is the explanation of what to adopt and what to abandon. However, it is unfortunate that most people engage only in worldly activities. Very few people engage in a regular practice of the Dharma; and very few, based on thorough and precise analysis, understand the perfect reasoning behind the Dharma. It seems that even if they do understand it somewhat, those who practice the

Dharma correctly and receive the resultant signs of reaching high levels of the path are even more rare—like stars in the daytime. We must understand, however, that this is due to faults of the people practicing the Dharma, not the Dharma itself. Again, the sacred Dharma is a method for living beings to subdue their own minds via a nonviolent, excellent path of gradually improving their conduct.

These days, material development and scientific technology are flourishing, but these advancements have brought an increase in conflict that disturbs our peace and happiness. In general, our thoughts and actions are becoming increasingly cruel, while as a society we are becoming spiritually poor. The worst troublemakers in the world appear to be human beings, as we engage in extremely negative actions, such as taking life on a vast scale, for the sake of our fleeting happiness. This is the nature of samsara.

When we experience pleasant situations, we feel attachment and desire for those pleasant feelings to endure. When we experience discomfort, we experience displeasure and anger that we must endure unpleasant conditions. As mentioned above, the source of both pleasure and displeasure is our own mind. Forgetting this is ignorance. That is why ignorance, according to Buddhism, is the fundamental source of all negative emotions, such as attachment and anger.

No matter how much we accumulate by way of worldly pleasure—or displeasure—it is impossible for these temporary states to bring us lasting happiness. Therefore, if we wish to attain liberation from endless suffering, we must elevate ourselves—our level of thinking and mental impulses—to accomplish buddhahood.

Although this may be difficult to achieve in a few years or even during our lifetime, it is important to persevere from now on and to make gradual progress. If we take the joyful path of training our mind, our life will be extremely meaningful, as a mind filled with bodhichitta will not deceive ourselves or others. To summarize:

If we abandon the two extremes, we are on the middle path
that is most praised by the great sage.
Distancing yourself from extreme views,
avoid falling strongly to either side.

I

The Four Noble Truths

After having attained perfect enlightenment at Bodhgaya, Buddha Shakyamuni walked slowly to Deer Park in Varanasi. There he first turned the profound wheel of the Dharma by teaching on the four noble truths to the five ascetics, his first retinue of perfect disciples.

When they saw the Buddha, the five ascetics offered him drinking water and told him that he looked like a noble being. In response to their offering, he said, "I am awake." In those three words the Buddha shared the essence of his teachings.

The Buddha advised his dear friends to understand *the truth of suffering*. Then he advised them to understand *the truth of the causes of suffering* and to abandon them. This he taught was *the truth of cessation* to be attained along the path. Finally, the Buddha advised them to rely on *the truth of the path* until liberation.

To understand the four noble truths, meditate upon this example: When you are sick, you must understand first what the disease is in order to heal it; this is equivalent to the truth of suffering. Then, after you know what the disease is, you need to understand what the causes of your sickness are; this is the investigation of the causes of suffering.

Then you ascertain that there is potential freedom from your ill health; this is the recognition that there is the cessation of suffering. Finally, to get well, there is the correct medicine that you need to take to regain your health, equivalent to the true path.

The teachings of the four noble truths are profoundly helpful because they relate directly to our own experience—to our natural desire to seek happiness and overcome suffering. If you understand the four noble truths, then you will understand the Buddha himself— as the way to examine a teacher is to examine his or her fundamental teachings. The Buddha gave his first teaching to help us eliminate suffering in our own lives and to help others attain the same liberation. This is the fundamental joy of the Buddhist path and why so many have chosen to follow the Buddha.

The First Noble Truth: The Truth of Suffering

The reason the Buddha taught suffering first is that its causes and conditions are like a disease. The cessation of suffering and its causes is likened to recovering happily from an illness, while a true path— meaning a genuine spiritual path—is similar to medicine that heals disease. If we do not recognize suffering first, we will not understand its causes and conditions. If we do not know what the causes and conditions of suffering are, there is no way to abandon them. How could we ever be happy without knowing the real truth of our condition? Therefore, the nature of suffering was taught first.

The two kinds of suffering—physical and mental—are summarized in the three aspects of suffering: suffering of suffering, suffering of change, and all-pervasive suffering of conditioning.

The suffering of suffering is the coarsest form, where before one type of suffering ends, another type of suffering arises. For example, we lose our job and then our house. This is the suffering of suffering.

The suffering of change is subtler. When things are subject to change, we experience this type of suffering. For example, when we are young, we have a healthy body with sharp senses. As we grow older, our eyes change so that it is more difficult to see clearly. This is the suffering of change.

The all-pervasive suffering of conditioning is the subtlest form—it doesn't appear to be suffering until you examine it further. For example, a pair of shoes seems to be a neutral object, not connected to any type of suffering. However, when we look at the shoe leather, we realize that living beings were harmed to produce those shoes.

These three types of suffering can be known directly through our own experience. When we start to think about suffering, we will feel uncomfortable. That uncomfortable feeling is important for our practice—when we practice compassion, understanding our own suffering and understanding others' suffering is the first step. Without that understanding we cannot practice compassion. To practice compassion, we need that uncomfortable feeling. Therefore, don't think that meditating upon suffering is dwelling in negativity. To understand the defects of samsara, we need a direct understanding of suffering.

What benefit is there in simply recognizing suffering? Recognizing that we have an illness will not help; we need to understand the source of the illness to cure it. Therefore, true causes, the basis from which all sufferings arise, are taught second.

The Second Noble Truth: The Cause of Suffering

The main cause of suffering is the karma of ignorance and its resulting mental afflictions. *Karma* is a Sanskrit word that means "action," and it implies that there is a cause for every action. Everything that we experience—happiness and unhappiness—is the result of past actions and causes. Karmic causes of suffering are impure actions of body, speech, and mind that reflect three types of karma: virtuous karma, unwholesome karma, and neutral karma. Our afflictions are principally caused by attachment, aversion, and ignorance. All phenomena that we experience arise from causes and conditions. It is important to think about how these experiences relate to cause and effect. If the cause is positive or negative, then either happiness or suffering results.

The Third Noble Truth: The Truth of Cessation

The Buddha taught us how to recognize both the presence of suffering and the cessation of suffering. If there were no possibility of cessation, then what would be the point of recognizing suffering? Once we understand the cause of suffering, then we may think about whether we can reduce its causes. By abandoning the causes of suffering we can realize the truth of cessation—liberation, which is nothing other than full realization of our true nature. Therefore, true cessation is taught third. Afflictions—our source of suffering—are not the nature of mind. The temporary stains of the afflictions can be separated from the mind. If we abandon these stains, we attain final liberation—true cessation—which is free from negative emotions and a permanent separation from all suffering caused by these afflictions.

The Fourth Noble Truth: The Truth of the Path

If you want to follow the Buddha, there are three paths that you may choose to practice: the Hinayana, the fundamental vehicle based on the first teachings of the Buddha; the Mahayana, based on the greater motivation of the buddhas and bodhisattvas to enlighten all beings; and the Vajrayana, which includes the Dzogchen teachings in the Nyingma lineage, the most advanced teachings on the union of skillful means and wisdom. Attaining freedom from all suffering depends on relying upon a correct path—because the truth of the path is the *method to attain liberation*. Therefore, the stages of the true path were taught fourth. These four noble truths are the foundation of all the Buddhist paths; they are the common ground for all vehicles.

Thus, with the four noble truths the Buddha shows us how to abandon unwanted suffering, including our afflictions and the karma that causes them, how to rely upon the antidote by which suffering is abandoned, and so forth. The great compassionate one, the Buddha, taught the sutras and tantras to liberate us from suffering and to establish us in the ultimate truth of the nature of reality.

Buddha Nature

There is only one element—one nature—and that is buddha nature. This basic goodness is our capacity to become fully awakened buddhas. Everyone possesses this buddha nature that each of us may find within ourselves. The *Samadhirajasutra* says,

> The essence of the sugatas pervades all beings.
> Generate the most vast and sublime of intentions,
> for each and every being has the cause of awakening—
> there is not a single sentient being who lacks this potential.

Buddhahood appears to be completely beyond all of us, due to the ignorance of our dualistic mind. Most beings never recognize their buddha nature; they don't even know that they have it. The Buddha says that there are two obstacles to recognition. The first obstacle is that many people don't wish to enter the path of enlightenment. The second is that many who enter the path do not complete it.

For many, their buddha nature is like a beautiful lotus growing in a north-facing cave that never receives the sunlight of the pointing-out instructions. This lotus dies without anyone enjoying its beauty. This is similar to us. We naturally possess many precious qualities, but we do not recognize them. We live our entire lives without seeing our beautiful buddha nature, our basic goodness. Therefore, we suffer continually with this ignorance—not knowing or enjoying our natural, pristine state—until we die. This is so sad!

As Nagarjuna says, if there is no gold in the ground, no matter how much you search for it, you will never find it. Similarly, if there is no buddha nature within us, then no matter how much we meditate, it will be impossible for us to attain liberation. However, enlightenment is in the palm of our hand because we do have the gold—the seed of buddha nature—within us. You might ask: If the essence of liberation is ever-present within us, why do we have so many obscurations? Why does our buddha nature not automatically eliminate all our obscurations?

The answer is that when temporary delusion arises in our own mind, in that moment we are unable to recognize the true nature of reality. Our primordial wisdom, the dharmakaya, clearly manifests at all times—evenly and without change. However, in the moment when delusion arises, we are unable to discover our true nature and recognize the way reality is. Our obscured wisdom is like a lotus flower that has not yet opened to the sunlight of reality.

Our buddha nature is unborn; this natural luminosity has existed as long as consciousness has existed, and consciousness has no beginning. It is for this reason that, in tantra, this subtle mind of luminosity (*ösel* in Tibetan) is called *unborn*. The Buddha stated that all beings possess buddha nature because he wanted us to know this truth. Knowing this, we can discover our buddha nature through meditation yoked to wisdom.

Maitreya's *Uttaratantrashastra* says that when buddha nature is obscured, one is an ordinary being. Later, when it is partially purified, that ordinary being becomes a bodhisattva. When buddha nature is completely realized, then the bodhisattva, who has freed him- or herself from all negativities, becomes a buddha. Therefore, three beings appear from one nature—what appears depends on the purity or power of their wisdom.

It is said that buddha nature is primordially pure. To understand this, you can use a teaching from the *Uttaratantrashastra*, reflecting upon the three examples of a gemstone, space, and water.

Buddha nature is like a gemstone. Although a gemstone is usually found within the ground, the stone itself is intrinsically untainted by the soil. Similarly, buddha nature is primordially pure. It has not been stained even for a moment by the dirt of disturbing emotions.

It is said that buddha nature is like space. The sky may be covered by clouds, but space itself remains pure and untouched by clouds. Similarly, our spacious, luminous buddha nature is unaffected by the delusions that temporarily obscure it.

Finally, it is said that buddha nature is like water. When dirt is mixed into water, the water becomes murky. However, the water itself can be purified. In the same way, although our negative emotions obscure our buddha nature, they are temporary and can be purified by following the stages of the path to enlightenment.

The *Uttaratantrashastra* explains this concept in detail through nine examples: a treasury of jewels hidden beneath a poor person's house, an ordinary woman who carries in her womb a child who will later become a great king, and so on. The general meaning of all these examples is that buddha nature is temporarily obscured by defilement, or negative emotions. As a result, the activities of a buddha cannot manifest.

Those who seek enlightenment naturally wish to purify their disturbing emotions to reveal their buddha nature. If you have this wish, know that at the beginning of the path, there will be many difficulties to overcome. For example, it is difficult not to desire things that are beautiful and attractive but do not ultimately contribute to our life's goal. It is hard not to get angry when you are insulted. It is difficult not to be disturbed by external conditions that disrupt your peace of mind. These disturbing emotions will make it difficult for you to discover your buddha nature. Despite this, because defilements are temporary and removable, you—and all living beings—have the potential to achieve enlightenment.

When your guru introduces you to the nature of mind, you will discover nothing other than what you already possess. You will know without doubt that your buddha nature is not your dualistic mind. If we stabilize the recognition of the wisdom pointed out to us by our teacher, then this wisdom will result in our attainment of true enlightenment in this very lifetime or in our future lives.

How do we do that? We make meditation on buddha nature our primary focus until we complete the stages of the path to enlightenment. Many great teachings on buddha nature are found in the Dzogchen tradition. One is Padmasambhava's *The Instruction of Pointing the Staff* that he gave to an old man who had great devotion to him. This instruction on the nature of mind is very beautiful in its simplicity, yet profound in its meaning:

> Listen here old man! Look into the awakened mind of your own awareness! It has neither form nor color, neither center nor edge. At first, it has no origin but is empty. Next, it has no dwelling place but is empty. At the end, it has no destination but is empty. This emptiness is not made of anything and is clear and cognizant. When you see this and recognize it, you know your natural face. You understand the nature of things. You have then seen the nature of mind, resolved the basic state of reality, and cut through doubts about topics of knowledge. This awakened mind of awareness is not made of any material substance; it is self-existing and inherent in yourself. This is the nature of things that is easy to realize because it is not to be sought for elsewhere. This is the nature of mind that does not consist of a concrete perceiver and something perceived to fixate on. It defies the limitations of permanence and annihilation. In it there is nothing to awaken; the awakened state of

enlightenment is your own awareness that is naturally awake. In it there is nothing that goes to the hells; awareness is naturally pure. In it there is no practice to carry out; its nature is naturally cognizant. This great view of the natural state is present in yourself: resolve that it is not to be sought for elsewhere.

The Nature of Reality

Whatever appears to our six sense faculties—visible forms, sounds, smells, tastes, textures, or mental objects—is relative. We must accept the valid conventional existence of the subjective and objective phenomena known to people in common. As Gendun Chöphel writes,

As soon as you live in this world, you believe in the unreal,
trusting what is false, developing many theories based on lies;
what else can you do?

However, when we analyze further, we realize that all phenomena lack inherent existence and are free from fabricated extremes of existence and nonexistence. The valid perception of realized noble beings tells us that the ultimate mode of existence of all phenomena is emptiness. As our extreme views of existence and nonexistence fall apart, we become aware that how things appear to us is mistaken and deceptive. The great meditator Kharakpa says,

All phenomena are like a dream or an illusion.
There is not even a single thing that is real.
Things appear while not existing.
So do not become attached to things!

If we are earnest and sincere in our Buddhist path, we must distance ourselves from deceptive states of mind to seek the ultimate truth.

When the true nature of reality manifests for realized beings, such as buddhas, the obscured, deceptive appearances of all phenomena—good, bad, and neutral—disappear completely. As Gendun Chöphel states,

> If we think that the dirt, mountains, and boulders as we see them now will still vividly appear just the same when we attain buddhahood, we are very mistaken. Grass may be very tasty to consciousness as long as that consciousness remains in the body of a donkey, but when consciousness emerges from that state, that taste for grass is also lost.

Until then, we, as ordinary people, remain completely deceived so long as our minds do not approach an understanding of the true nature of phenomena. We must correct our mind's way of perceiving. Whatever our dualistic mind perceives is merely a conceptual, superficial experience of the relative mind that experiences subjective and objective phenomena.

In contrast, our natural awareness (*rigpa*) is without dualistic thinking. Whatever is experienced within the nonconceptual wakefulness of natural awareness is correctly perceived. Natural awareness experiences reality as it truly is. However, until we recognize the knowing quality of our mind, our perceptions are mistaken.

The teachings of the Buddha describe reality in two ways: the relative—how things appear; and the ultimate—how things truly are. These two states of mind—the conceptual mind and the nonconceptual wakefulness of natural awareness—are the basis of the suffering of samsara and the liberation of nirvana, respectively.

Phenomena and their ultimate nature (*dharmata*) exist together within the same base, but how they appear differs, depending on whether we recognize natural awareness. The entirety of samsara and nirvana have one common ground. From that one ground the two paths of *not knowing* and *knowing*—in Tibetan, *marigpa* and *rigpa*— lead to two results: samsara and nirvana, respectively. This fundamental basis of the ground is great emptiness (*shunyata*). Who has that base? You have it, we have it, all living beings have it. Our mind, our body, and the entire universe merge into this great emptiness. It is the pervasive nature of all living beings.

The path to samsara begins with ignorance, or not knowing (*marigpa*); the path to nirvana begins with the wisdom of self-liberation, or knowing (*rigpa*). Ignorance and self-liberation are similar to an electric light switch. If you turn off a light, you have the darkness of ignorance. If you turn it on, you have the luminosity of recognition. With recognition, you have nirvana; without recognition, you have samsara. For example, if we recognize the interdependence of all phenomena appearing out of emptiness, we know the nature of reality. Not knowing this is fundamental ignorance—this is the cause of all our suffering. *The Prayer of Samantabhadra* begins with three stanzas that point out the view of natural awareness:

All that appears and exists—all of samsara and nirvana—has one ground, two paths, and two results. It is a miraculous display of knowing and not knowing. Through *The Prayer of Samantabhadra*, may all beings realize perfect enlightenment in the expanse of the dharmadhatu.

The ground of all is uncompounded, a self-arisen, infinite, and inconceivable expanse, having neither the name samsara nor nirvana. If it is known, buddhahood is attained. If it is not known, beings wander in samsara. May all beings of the three realms realize the nature of the inexpressible ground.

I, Samantabhadra, recognized from the beginning the nature of the ground—free from cause and condition—that is this spontaneously arisen self-awareness. It is without the defect of affirming or denying the outer or the inner. It is not hidden by the darkness of mindlessness; thus, self-appearance is unobscured.

2

Interdependence

Understanding interdependence requires understanding cause and effect (known as karma), as all external objects and internal aggregates are merely relatively existent. The word *karma* means "action" and refers specifically to the process of cause and effect related to actions and their consequences. The founder of Buddhism, Buddha Shakyamuni, was a human being who suffered just as we do. When he was twenty-nine, he left his royal family to search for a way to end his and other living beings' suffering. He studied meditation with many teachers, and after six years of practice, he had a profound breakthrough and became a buddha—one who is filled with understanding. The Buddha explains,

> I have seen deeply that nothing can be by itself alone—that
> everything depends on each other. And also I have seen that
> all beings are capable—possessing the nature of awakening.

The pinnacle of all views is dependent origination (*pratityasamutpada*), which is the correct understanding of how things exist and the mind that apprehends them to exist in that way. All external and internal phenomena come into existence in dependence upon causes and conditions. If we realize that all relative phenomena are dependently arisen and do not truly exist by themselves, we rid ourselves of harmful confusion, ignorance, and wrong views that grasp at an inherent self—and we take an important step toward purifying our karma.

Everything is contingent on cause and condition. *Cause* refers to a preceding object that has the power to produce or the potential to become another object. *Condition* refers to that which accompanies a cause and has the power to affect the result by increasing it, decreasing it, and so forth. It is through the coming together of causes and conditions that outer and inner phenomena come into being, and it is through the meeting of causes and conditions that pleasant and unpleasant feelings arise.

Our own states of being—happiness and sadness—arise in dependence upon causes and conditions. They are not without cause, not permanent, not arisen from a creator outside of the field of interdependence, and so on. Also, they do not arise from a single cause or a single condition. They arise from the meeting of many causes and conditions. In particular, they arise in dependence upon and relative to other living beings and other phenomena. Knowing this, we recognize that our well-being is related to the well-being of all beings. For us to be genuinely happy, we must act for the happiness of all. This is genuinely important to know and understand.

Chandrakirti teaches that the reasoning of dependent origination cuts through the net of all wrong views. When we correctly understand the view of dependent origination, we will understand the emptiness of all phenomena and the fact that karmic cause and effect is unfailing. This wisdom dispels the erroneous views of permanence and nihilism, causing us to become relaxed and open-minded.

Whoever we are, whether or not we accept the notion of karma, we have the suffering of birth, sickness, aging, and death. Everything that we experience is the result of our past karma. That is why we must take responsibility for our actions. It is not possible for karmic causes to wear out naturally so that we do not have to experience the ripening of their effects. We are responsible for our experiences—our karma.

Any action carried out with an afflicted state of mind creates a seed that will ripen into a similar result. Our karma arises from mental afflictions of two types: conceptual afflictions, such as mistaken views; and emotional afflictions, such as ignorance, attachment, aversion, pride, and jealousy. When these five poisons arise in our mind, they disturb us and cause deep unhappiness.

Thus, karma accumulates in the mind based on our actions of body, speech, and mind; karma involves *cause and effect, time,* and *action*. Our individual actions may be completely positive, completely negative, or a mixture of positive and negative. This is true of collective karma as well.

Collective karma accumulates as a result of group actions, such as the negative actions of soldiers killing during times of war or the positive actions of spiritual practitioners meditating together. Group karma is experienced as a collective, but each individual in a group thinks, speaks, and acts a little bit differently, so individuals will experience the results of war and group meditation differently.

Sometimes the results of karmic consequences do not appear immediately. As with a bird flying deep into the sky, there will be no shadow. But sooner or later the bird must land; when it does, its shadow is there. This is what we call hidden karma, which can be very difficult to understand.

In the Buddhist tradition, we say that negative actions motivated by the ego's self-grasping result in nonvirtue, whereas positive actions motivated by selflessness result in virtue. Virtue, which ensures our individual and collective happiness, depends completely on having a good heart filled with love, kindness, and compassion for all living beings—*bodhichitta*—as the motivation for all our actions of body, speech, and mind. From the Mahayana point of view, delusion refers to our mistaken grasping at a nonexistent self. Therefore, understanding the heart of enlightenment, the cultivation of bodhichitta, is profoundly important.

Karma in Daily Life

If you think that Buddhism says that everything is suffering and we cannot do anything about it, you are actually stating the opposite of the Buddha's teaching. Suffering doesn't come from nowhere; it arises as a result of its own causes and conditions. If we do not realize the power of our mind, we naturally will harm others. All suffering is caused by our mind. When our mind is peaceful and virtuous, even our physical body looks pleasing and beautiful.

If we mix our worldly activities with the kind mind of bodhichitta, we can accomplish our daily activities in a capable, virtuous way. Repeatedly check your motivation upon waking, upon going to sleep, and at all times in between. In this way, you can maintain mindfulness to ensure that you are conducting your daily life with bodhichitta mind. A good motivation, a kind heart, is what we must have all the time. This, and nothing else, is the primary Dharma practice given to us by our gurus. Indeed, bodhichitta is our heart guru.

Make a promise to yourself in the morning to dedicate your actions to the benefit of all living beings. Try not to harm anyone. If you have the capacity to help someone, do it. This is the best way to start your day. Be mindful during the day of your thoughts and emotions. Let your thoughts, speech, and actions reflect your kind mind—your bodhichitta motivation. If you notice negative thoughts or emotions arising, practice their antidotes or allow them to self-liberate—to disappear on their own without furthering them.

Remember: if we show others love and respect, they will respond in kind, thereby increasing happiness for all. If we show others anger and hatred, we cause negative emotions to arise, increasing unhappiness for all. According to Nagarjuna, actions arising from attachment, aversion, and ignorance are negative; actions arising from the absence of these are positive. This is the key thing to remember.

Sometimes my students are confused when despite cultivating bodhichitta, meditating, and dedicating their lives to helping others, they experience sickness and other problems.

This also happened to the Buddha when he was about to reach enlightenment and his final obstacles—personified as a demon called Mara—that he needed to recognize and go beyond arose. First, the demon of desire arose with the appearance of beautiful, seductive women called the daughters of Mara. The demon of anger arose as Mara tried to engage him in a fight with weapons. The Buddha did not respond to these unpleasant demons or projections of his ego, but instead he practiced the kind mind of bodhichitta. Thus, he became enlightened by overcoming his final obstacles. As students of the Buddha, we always look to this example to recognize that we can use obstacles in our life on our path toward enlightenment. We can use our problems as opportunities to practice bodhichitta.

If you experience this, it is a good sign that you are purifying your negative karma within this lifetime. When problems arise, view them as signs of the power of your practice—manifestations of negative karma that are ripening and coming to completion now. You will not have to experience their adverse effects in the future.

Every action has an effect that will ripen either in this lifetime, in a future one, or at an indefinite time. There are various ways that effects ripen. Generally, the first results we experience have the biggest effect, either positive or negative. If there are many actions that are equal, those most closely related to our state of mind at death or our strongest habitual tendencies are the ones we experience first. Finally, results typically arise chronologically, with the oldest arising first and the newest arising last. It depends, however, on how we accumulate our karma. In any case, the ripening is inevitable once the karmic seed has been planted.

You will experience the results of your individual and collective karma. The Buddha cannot change your karma. However, by following the Buddha's teachings, you can diminish your negative karma from the past and prevent your negative karma from arising in the future. It is up to you. As the Buddha says in the *Damamukanidanasutra*,

> Do not disregard small misdeeds,
> thinking they are harmless,
> because even tiny sparks of flame
> can set fire to a mountain of hay.

> Do not disregard small positive acts,
> thinking they are without benefit,
> because even tiny drops of water
> will eventually fill a large container.

Karma works with precision—good results from good; bad results from bad. That is how it works. Knowing this, what should we do? We should try to benefit others and try not to harm them. The Buddha said that violent people, those who harm sentient beings, were not his followers. *The Application of Mindfulness Sutra* says,

> Through virtue, happiness is obtained.
> From nonvirtue, suffering befalls you.
> Accordingly, the karma and results of
> Virtue and nonvirtue are clearly taught.

3

Introduction to Meditation

Meditation is the primary method we use to transform our mind to be more compassionate and connected with our buddha nature, the true nature of reality. The Tibetan word for meditation, *gom*, means "to become familiar with an object by concentrating on it." The object of our meditation can be anything but mainly it is the mind itself, as this is the root of everything.

As Buddhists, we believe that all our actions are dependent on the state of our mind. An uncontrolled mind can cause a great deal of harm, while a peaceful mind can create a sense of profound well-being. Meditation is important because it serves to harmonize the body and the mind as well as to create a balanced state of inner and outer peace. Meditation is a practice that makes it possible to culti-vate and develop natural human qualities, such as bodhichitta and wisdom, in the same way that other types of training make it possible to play a musical instrument or acquire any other skill.

Meditation helps us to familiarize ourselves with a clear and true way of seeing things and to cultivate the positive qualities of our buddha nature that would remain otherwise dormant or undeveloped within us. The ultimate reason for meditating is to transform ourselves in order to transform our world in a more beneficial way. To put it another way, we transform ourselves so that we can become better human beings and serve others with wisdom and skillful means. That is why we need to meditate.

The goal of meditation is not to shut down the mind but rather to make it free, clear, and balanced. When we choose an object of meditation that triggers positive thoughts in our mind, then our state of mind will become peaceful. If we choose an object that gives us negative feelings, our mind will feel depressed. Since we meditate to achieve something positive, it is important to choose an uplifting object. Generally there are two types of meditation: single-pointed concentration meditation and analytical meditation. When we practice concentration, we focus our mind on an object and remain there with no distractions. If our body is in a perfect meditation posture but our mind is thinking about objects of attachment or anger, then we are not meditating with single-pointed concentration. Single-pointed concentration is also the basis for the analytical meditation that is necessary to discover the final true nature of our mind and phenomena.

Recognition of the true nature of mind and phenomena, in turn, is a prerequisite to achieving enlightenment. Enlightenment is a state beyond human understanding and free from any form of negativity or ignorance. In that state, every perfect condition is naturally present—perfect love, compassion, knowledge, and happiness. This is the true nature of all beings. Our enlightenment depends on not only the Buddha showing us the way but also our practice of meditation. Enlightenment cannot be achieved without practice or by practicing the wrong path.

If you wish to meditate, you must first receive instruction from a qualified guru who has attained results from his or her practice. In this way, you establish that the teacher's lineage and meditation practice are authentic and suitable for you to follow. It is good that many people teach meditation; however, as the great master Patrul Rinpoche advises, we should examine the level of understanding of these teachers. Also, some people think that they can create their own way to meditate and don't need to learn from a qualified teacher, but they risk following the wrong path. They won't have the oral instructions and personal guidance of their teacher, which results in a greater chance of unnecessary obstacles arising that will eventually cause the student to lose their enthusiasm and give up their meditation practice. This, of course, means that they won't achieve the results in the short and long term.

To control our mind, we must develop the three wisdoms—listening, contemplating, and meditating. The Buddha advises us to begin by listening to the teachings and to develop our understanding by studying them. In the *Bodhisattvapitaka* he says,

Through study we come to understand phenomena.
Through study we turn away from negative actions.
Through study we give up what is meaningless.
Through study we reach the state beyond sorrow.

Then through meditation we integrate what we have learned in our training until we experience unconditional love, compassion, bodhichitta, and enlightenment. That is the meaning and purpose of meditation.

When you meditate, first pay attention to gathering the proper physical, mental, and environmental causes and conditions; then engage in the practice without agitation and anxiety. If you find that uncomfortable circumstances, either inner or outer, are arising repeatedly when you meditate, you must ask your spiritual teacher for help. If you deal with these circumstances quickly, they will be easily dispelled by following the advice of your guru. Beginners should not develop too many expectations when they practice. Accept both good and bad experiences, and practice continually without attachment or worries.

Due to the activity of their body's subtle channels, energies, and essences, some students have extraordinary experiences when they practice. What these students experience is neither amazing nor wrong but just unique to their experience. If you hear sounds, see lights, or experience unusual feelings or thoughts, you should neither identify with them nor become conceptually involved with them, regardless of whether they appear to be helpful or harmful. If they appear to be good visions, don't label them as auspicious. If they appear to be negative, don't become depressed. Just let them be and maintain the object of your awareness. *This is a very important point.*

If you identify with these distractions from your object of meditation, your practice may become increasingly difficult, as you will habitually experience them again and again. When you hear a noise, for example, just let it pass. Do not identify with it and don't conceptually elaborate on it. Just hear it and immediately go back to focusing on your object of meditation, maintaining the clarity of your mind.

Cultivate a sense of equanimity and acceptance in the face of whatever occurs in your meditation. For example, if you find your meditation is going very well and your concentration is good, do not be filled with great pride. If, on the other hand, your concentration is bouncing all over, do not be depressed or worry. Maintain equanimity and accept all meditation experiences as they arise without being too tight or too loose.

The Three Supreme Methods

There are three supreme methods that should accompany your meditation at all times. They pertain to how you start your meditation, how you maintain your practice, and how you finish your session.

When you meditate, first give rise to your bodhichitta motivation, inseparable from your love and compassion for all living beings. Then enter meditative concentration inseparable from mindfulness and alert awareness. If you become tired when meditating, rest. Finally, at the end of your session, when you emerge from your meditative concentration—without leaving your physical meditation posture—reflect on the fact that living beings in samsara do not understand such profound Dharma practice and therefore fall under the influence of their delusions. Due to this, they experience continuous suffering, day and night.

Then, for the sake of these living beings, aspire not to fall prey to laziness. Determine to develop your mind's meditative concentration until you attain the state of enlightenment. Meditate briefly on compassion for all living beings in this way and then evaluate your meditation session. If it went well, rejoice and be glad. If it was a poor session of meditation, do not become discouraged—resolve to improve your future sessions. How an experienced meditator evaluates their sessions is based on how well they followed the objective of the meditation practice. For example, if you are practicing compassion meditation, then your mind should be transformed by the practice. If you are not experiencing any changes in your mind, then your meditation sessions are not effective.

To go into depth on each of these three supreme methods, we can see that by correcting your motivation and generating bodhichitta, you will benefit others through whatever you do—ensuring that your actions become a source of good. Do this by reminding yourself that there is not a single being in samsara—this immense ocean of suffering—who is free from torment. Remind yourself that it is for their well-being that you practice the profound Dharma. It is important to have this attitude each time you start your meditation practice.

In the middle, maintain your pure view by practicing with a mind free from conceptualization; practice without distraction and without losing your focus. If you allow many thoughts to arise, they will destroy your inner peace, and you will lose your main practice. Whatever type of meditation you do, concentrate single-pointedly with mindfulness so that the merit of your practice will not be destroyed by circumstances, such as by anger or other disturbing emotions.

Finally, it is very important to finish the session with a seal of dedication and prayers to benefit others. At the end of your session, if you have done anything that is good or virtuous, you should dedicate the merit of that for the sake of all. The essence of dedicating the merit is to visualize that all your good deeds will be of benefit to all living beings. Start by thinking about all the virtuous things you have done in the past, all the good things that you are doing now, and all the beneficial things you will do in the future. Then bring all that together in union with the merit generated by the buddhas of the past, present, and future. This is the same dedication method that all the buddhas and bodhisattvas used in the past. This is how you should seal your meditation session. Remember these three supreme methods whenever you meditate.

In your subsequent conduct, be generous to sentient beings; practice patience as taught in the commentaries on the six paramitas, such as Patrul Rinpoche's *Words of My Perfect Teacher*; and persevere in gathering the two accumulations of merit and wisdom. The six paramitas are the ways that a bodhisattva trains in cultivating the virtues on the path toward enlightenment, starting with generosity and culminating in the wisdom of enlightenment. The first five paramitas are how one accumulates merit, and the sixth paramita is the perfection of wisdom, which is the accumulation of wisdom itself.

GUIDED MEDITATION ON THE THREE
PRECEPTS OF BODY, SPEECH, AND MIND

In Buddhism, the three precepts are fundamental as they help to unify our body, speech, and mind to prevent distractions from arising during a meditation session.

The Body Precept: Meditation Posture

To quickly develop realization in our mind, we, as followers of the Buddha, should first emulate his meditation posture. His cross-legged posture is called the *seven-point meditation posture of Vairochana*. When he attained enlightenment under the bodhi tree at Vajrasana in Bodhgaya, the Buddha was sitting this way, as it makes the channels (*nadi*) and winds (*prana*) of our subtle-energy body optimal for meditation.

To meditate in this posture, first sit on a meditation cushion with your legs crossed—either with both ankles in full lotus or one ankle in half lotus resting on your thighs, whichever is most comfortable. If you are not capable of sitting cross-legged on the floor or if you are unwell or infirm, sit in a chair. Second, place your hands below your navel in the gesture (*mudra*) of meditative equipoise—your palms facing up, right hand over left; or you may stretch out both palms facing downward to cover your knees in the gesture of elemental mind at ease. Third, it is important for your spine to be straight and upright like an arrow—not arched backward or bent forward—so that your mind and the flow of your subtle energy are natural. Fourth, leave your shoulders even and relaxed. Fifth, tuck your chin down slightly toward your Adam's apple without holding your head too high or too low or tilting it to the right or left. Sixth, leave your teeth and lips natural, placing the tip of your tongue lightly against your upper palate. Seventh, cast your gaze—with your eyes not too widely open or too tightly closed—down toward the tip of your nose. This completes the seven points of the posture.

If keeping your eyes open makes you unable to stay focused because you are distracted by external objects, close your eyes slightly. Once your visualization is clear, gradually open them.

If in closing your eyes different colored lights—such as red and white—appear, your mind may be too focused on your visual consciousness or your eyes may be too tightly closed. Abandoning these mistakes, it is important to settle your attention naturally on your mind itself. Breathe gently without agitation or making a loud noise. It is important that your breathing be slow, relaxed, and imperceptible.

Many good qualities come from sitting in this seven-point posture, as it naturally supports your meditation. If your body remains straight, upright, and relaxed, the mind and the subtle energies remain natural. If the body is straight, the channels— the nadi—are straight. If the channels are straight, the energies flow straight and smoothly. If the winds—the prana—are smooth, the mind remains naturally settled and does not wander about, following thoughts. To summarize, as Patrul Rinpoche states, when meditating there are three things you should remember: place your body on your seat, your mind in your body, and relaxation in your mind. I love this advice from Patrul Rinpoche. These three instructions are indispensable for practitioners.

The Speech Precept: Clearing the Channels

The speech precept is clearing the channels of the subtle-energy body through breath-related exercises. To perform what is called the *nine-round breathing exercise*, sit in the seven-point posture or on a chair, extend the four fingers of your left hand and press your thumb against the base of your ring finger. Keep your index finger extended but close the remaining three fingers over your left thumb.

With your extended index finger, block your left nostril and slowly expel the stale energies from your right nostril three times, clearing the right channel. While doing this, visualize that you are expelling all your own and others' bad karma, obscurations, and imprints accumulated from beginningless lifetimes due to anger and hatred, as well as all unwanted physical sickness and mental suffering.

Then, with your index finger of your right hand, block your right nostril and exhale the stale energies slowly from your left nostril three times, clearing the left channel. While doing this, visualize that you are expelling all your own and others' bad karma, obscurations, and imprints accumulated from beginningless lifetimes due to attachment.

Finally, placing your palms facing downward on your knees, sit up straight and clear the stale energies through both nostrils three times, clearing the central channel. While doing this, visualize that all your own and others' bad karma, obscurations, and imprints accumulated from beginningless lifetimes due to ignorance and confusion are cleared and purified.

Perform a total of nine rounds of clearing the stale energies: three with the left channel, three with the right channel, and three with the central channel. You may also clear the stale energies by first expelling from the right nostril for one breath, then from the left nostril for one breath, and finally from both nostrils for one breath. Repeat the entire cycle three times.

Practice: Blessing Impure Lung

An exercise described in the oral transmission lineage of the gurus instructs that all impure karma and deluded energies should be blessed by the seed syllables OM, ĀH, and HŪM, which are, respectively, the nature of the body, speech, and mind of all the buddhas.

To visualize this, breathe in naturally and visualize your inhalation as a white OM: ༀ. As your breath remains inside your body, visualize it as a red ĀḤ: ᔦ. Finally, when exhaling, visualize it as a blue HŪṂ: ₹.

Practice: Vase Breathing (Lung Bumchen)

For the practice known as vase breathing, sit in the seven-point posture as before. First, inhale slowly and gently through both nostrils and hold the upper energies below your navel while squeezing the lower energies upward.

Press the upper and lower energies together. Holding the vase breath, keep your abdomen completely filled for as long as you can. With circular movements, rotate your abdomen to the right three times; then rotate your abdomen to the left three times; and exhale completely. The visualizations are the same as those done with cleansing your breath explained above.

This is very beneficial for preventing disease and alleviating indigestion. As a means for the body and mind to remain at peace, it is particularly important as an indispensable preliminary for beginning meditators. There are many ways of clearing the stale energies, so you should experiment to see which method is most helpful for you; it is not necessary to practice them all.

The Mind Precept: Adjusting Motivation

The mind precept requires adjusting your motivation. After the subtle energies are flowing smoothly and naturally, rest your mind and body, leaving your awareness natural. Then turn inward, examine your mind, and adjust your motivation.

This is even more important than the instructions of the first and second precepts, as your body is like the servant of everything that is virtuous or not, while your mind is like a king with control over all. The motivation is, as explained before, precious bodhichitta, an extremely vast intention to benefit yourself and others. As Khenchen Padma Tsewang teaches,

With supreme bodhichitta induced by compassion,
simply put effort into taming your own wild mind!

We must try to develop impartial, great compassion for all beings. The best method to develop this good motivation of bodhichitta is to understand how all sentient beings are of great benefit to us in our life. Without living beings, how could we meditate on the love, compassion, and bodhichitta that allow us to practice the teachings of the Buddha and attain liberation? How could we eliminate all defilements and obtain all the realizations of the Mahayana without depending on others? Living beings are the foundation of our practice and the cause of true happiness and enjoyment. All happiness that we experience depends on others and comes to us through their kindness.

Realizing this, the Buddha discovered that the practice of bodhichitta is profound, and he made this precious teaching available to anyone who wishes to practice it. As we meditate on bodhichitta, the Buddha's qualities are developed in our mind in dependence upon others, and we eventually become living buddhas.

Living beings are very kind to us in worldly terms as well. We can only achieve worldly aims—praise and veneration, fame and renown, and wealth and enjoyments—in dependence upon them. The slightest good quality or happiness arises in dependence upon others and cannot arise without them. Keeping this in mind, it is not difficult to develop the compassionate intention of precious bodhichitta in our worldly and spiritual lives.

Mind is primary, controlling all gross and subtle activities. Therefore, we must primarily transform and develop our mind. In fact, the main reason for the Buddha's teachings and the intended result of our Dharma practice is for our mind to change in a positive way—for our mind to take the excellent path of internal transformation. Therefore, whenever we begin any activity, it is very important to adjust our motivation toward a positive direction.

Our motivation has two stages: self-interest and altruism. Here, selfishness—self-cherishing—is an improper motivation. A pure motivation is the wish to eliminate our own faults in order to benefit others. The supreme motivation is the wish to serve the happiness of all beings without hope of receiving anything in return.

The Tibetan word *kun-lhong*—meaning motivation—has two syllables: *kun* means "all," referring to the many positive, negative, and neutral thoughts that incessantly arise; and *lhong* means to select the most important of those thoughts to cultivate.

If we do not have good motivation, it doesn't matter how hard we work with our body or speech—not much good will come of it. Without the motivation of bodhichitta, without renouncing delusion and aspiring for awakening, if we just want protection from danger or for benefit to ourselves, any physical or verbal austerities that we undertake will not be powerful, virtuous, or positive, as these are not supreme motivations. As Rigdzin Jigme Lingpa says, the reflected images of virtue or non-virtue are cast by nothing but good or bad intentions.

If we do not have the motivation of renunciation and bodhichitta, and if our motivation is only focused on this life, then even if we meditate on the highest tantric practices of the nonconceptual awareness of *mahasandhi* or *mahamudra*, it will only be an imitation of virtue. To purely and correctly practice the Dharma, we must have an excellent motivation. Without this, we can attempt any practice whatsoever, but there will be no benefit. This is stated very clearly in the sutras and tantras.

So how do we understand what correct motivation is and practice with it? Start by thinking about yourself and others, remembering that we all have negative thoughts and karma. These are the root of our suffering. According to Buddhism, we all desire happiness and do not want suffering. Therefore, we say that we should always take care of our minds and try to help others. As I stated earlier, if we are able to help others, then we should. If we are unable to help others, we should at least not harm them.

It is essential to understand your own capacity to help others. Helping others doesn't mean merely doing great deeds. Whatever your capacity, help others when you can. For instance, when you see insects while walking, put them in a safe place off the road and say some prayers for them. This is how you start to help other living beings and gradually develop your capacity to do great deeds. To accomplish this, you need to cultivate compassion and bodhichitta—the wish that others be free from suffering and the desire to help them not to suffer. As Gendun Chöphel writes,

The ant, without eyes, races toward happiness.
Worms, without feet, race toward happiness.
In short, the whole world lines up to race toward
     happiness,
each faster than the other.

Just like you, everyone wants happiness and wishes to avoid suffering. Through understanding this, you can develop compassion for all beings and increase your bodhichitta mind. Seeing no difference between yourself and others, you begin to develop equanimity. Once you start this process of developing your bodhichitta mind, you will understand that you do not have the desire to harm others and that you do desire to help them not to suffer. This is the goal of your meditation. For this reason, we practice developing bodhichitta.

All living beings have the potential to attain enlightenment. What is the reason, from the Buddhist point of view, to obtain liberation from suffering? The answer is very clear. If you develop the mind of bodhichitta, you recognize that all beings have the potential to awaken and to benefit countless living beings. Bodhichitta is the fervent and profound wish to attain full enlightenment in order to help all living beings fully awaken to their buddha nature. Although attaining enlightenment is the motivation for Buddhists to practice meditation, meditation can be practiced by anyone. Because everyone has a mind, we can all work with our motivation and our mind via meditation.

We need to understand with certainty that creating positive karma with its resultant happiness, as opposed to creating negative karma with its resultant suffering, depends solely on having the motivation of renunciation and bodhichitta. As Patrul Rinpoche summarizes in *The Words of My Perfect Teacher*,

> This development of bodhichitta in the mind is the combined essence of all of Buddha's 84,000 collections of teachings. With it one is supreme. Without it one is unfortunate. It is the panacea for hundreds of ills. All other Dharma paths, such as the two accumulations, the purification of defilements, meditation on deities and recitation of mantras, are simply methods to make this wish-granting gem, bodhichitta, take birth in the mind. Without bodhichitta, none of them can lead you to the level of perfect buddhahood on their own. With bodhi-

chitta as your motivation, whatever Dharma practice you do becomes a cause for the attainment of buddhahood. At all times and occasions, train in numerous methods solely to develop bodhichitta alone.

Therefore, it is extremely important to strive enthusiastically in your mind to develop renunciation and bodhichitta. Once you have these as a foundation, all other good mental qualities will arise automatically without effort. Whether or not you are a Dharma practitioner is determined solely by whether you have renunciation and bodhichitta in your mind.

Most people think that the difference between being a Buddhist or not is based on taking refuge vows. But that is not the main point. The main point is your motivation for taking the vows. When you take refuge vows, if your primary motivation is one of renunciation—fiercely wishing to attain liberation from samsara—then your vows are based on the foundational vehicle, the Hinayana. When you take refuge vows, if your primary motivation is one of bodhichitta—taking them for the sake of all sentient beings—then your vows are based on the great vehicle of the Mahayana. Investigate your reasons for taking refuge vows. If you have taken refuge vows without these two motivations—just for protection from danger or wishing for a good worldly life—how could that be a complete vow of refuge? You must understand definitively that these two motivations are continually important for our practice—at the beginning, middle, and end.

The Three People and One Tsatsa

If your motivation is truly compassionate and good, any action that you perform becomes virtuous. Even if the action appears unwholesome, if it is well motivated it is actually virtuous. This is illustrated, for example, by the story of how three people attained enlightenment on the basis of a *tsatsa*, a sacred small clay statue of a buddha, that they found on the side of a road.

It is said that someone made a tsatsa and placed it on the side of a road. A person passing by thought that the tsatsa would quickly be destroyed by the rain, so they placed a shoe over it to shelter it from the rain. Later, another person walked by and thought that there could be no worse fault than placing a filthy shoe over a tsatsa, so they removed the shoe. Through the making, covering, and uncovering of the tsatsa, all three people, through the power of their good motivation, created the positive karma temporarily to enjoy higher rebirths in samsara and ultimately attain the highest liberation.

A great motivation allows all your actions to become the cause of enlightenment and the cause of happiness for all beings—that is the purpose of the Dharma. Therefore, you should lead your life with the thought of benefiting all beings. In Buddhism, this is the great motivation of generating bodhichitta, which is the heart of enlightenment.

For example, if you recite a Vajrasattva mantra once with the great motivation of bodhichitta, you get the same benefit as you would from reciting one hundred thousand mantras without bodhichitta motivation. The amount of purification you get from meditating on Vajrasattva doesn't depend on how many mantras you recite but on their quality. Of course, the number has power, but the quality of your recitation is more important. Similarly, if you offer one candle with the great motivation of bodhichitta, you get the same amount of merit as you do from offering one hundred thousand candles without it. And if you donate a small amount of money to a person with the great motivation of bodhichitta, you get the same amount of merit as you do from donating a large sum without it.

If you perform all actions with a good motivation, then one day you will reach buddhahood, as that is the result of your good motivation and positive actions. Make sure to correct your motivation before acting. If you cannot transform your motivation, don't perform the action until you can.

Since everything depends upon your motivation, at the beginning of your Dharma activities, first you should keep your body, speech, and mind natural. You should acknowledge that you have attained something very difficult to obtain—you have a precious human life that is the special basis for the practice of the Dharma. Second, acknowledge that you have encountered sacred teachers and the precious teachings of the Buddha, which are extremely rare and hard to find. Third, take a moment to appreciate that you have developed the rare wish to practice the Dharma. Fourth, be grateful that all your faculties and the conditions conducive to your Dharma practice are present.

Once you recognize the preciousness of these four rare conditions, it is very important to promise yourself from the depths of your heart that you will not waste this opportunity. As Khenchen Tsultrim Lodrö comments,

> Having the fortune to journey a single time into the
> human realm, even if I enjoy everything I need, it is no
> great wonder. But to have the good fortune to meet
> this path of the Dharma that can't be found for many
> eons—that makes me truly joyful!

Thus, as you encounter the Buddha's teachings and meditate on the difficulty of obtaining your precious human life with its freedoms and opportunities to practice the sacred Dharma, you should make a promise to practice virtue at your earliest opportunity, recognizing that your life is impermanent. You have attained such perfect conditions for your Dharma practice by having previously created the perfect causes for it. You should, in all situations, maintain the intention to powerfully benefit yourself and others.

The Criteria for Benefiting Beings

It is important to reflect upon what brings happiness into our daily life and what gives the most meaning to our life. The bodhisattvas are great human beings who do nothing but act for the benefit of beings, either directly or indirectly. In contrast, ordinary beings make mistakes, no matter how good their intentions might be. Ordinary beings might not benefit beings and could actually be a direct or indirect cause of harm because they lack wisdom. Therefore, understanding the criteria for how to act for others' benefit is very important. Patrul Rinpoche gave us teachings about when we should and should not act for the benefit of others. These teachings increase our wisdom so that we can act properly.

Patrul Rinpoche advises that if any activity directly or indirectly benefits ourselves or others, we must perform it. If there is no benefit, do not do it. If an action benefits ourselves but harms others, do not do it. If an action benefits others slightly but harms ourselves greatly, do not do it. However, if an action is beneficial to others and harmful to ourselves to an equal degree, we should undertake it, depending on the situation.

He advises against performing actions for a lesser good—for example, we should not harm a human being to benefit an animal. Likewise, if an action benefits many living beings yet harms a few, we should do it for the greater good. The reverse is also true—if an action harms many living beings and benefits only a few, we should not do it. We should always try to protect living beings from harm, if possible—

this includes ourselves. If an action benefits this life but harms our future life, we shouldn't do it. If an action harms this life but benefits future lives, we should perform the action.

If we have a pure bodhichitta mind, then even if an action appears unwholesome but it directly or indirectly benefits others, we should perform it. For instance, in some circumstances we should lie in order to save the lives of beings; take someone's life out of love and compassion, if they are going to harm many living beings; steal to give to the oppressed and destitute; or temporarily give teachings on the provisional meaning of the Buddha's teachings in order to guide students to the definitive meaning. These actions may appear negative; however, they are actually virtuous. For example, in Tibet, many families are nomadic herders of yak, sheep, and horses. If one of these animals is hurt by a predator, the herders may decide out of compassion to kill the animal to prevent it from suffering, if it is going to die anyway. This is an example of mercy killing that may appear negative but is not because of the bodhichitta motivation.

The most important point is to perform actions for the sake of living beings with bodhichitta based on the wisdom of what benefits living beings most greatly. As Shantideva says,

Don't sacrifice greatly for a small purpose.
Emphasize primarily the welfare of others.

The Value of Human Life

The Buddha said that a human life is a gift beyond measure and a great blessing. Knowing this, we must identify what our objectives are for our lives. If we are attached to the pleasures of this life alone and ignore the happiness of other beings, if we harm them and act like butchers to destroy their happiness, how sad and unskillful—how serious the harm! Khenchen Tsultrim Lodrö admonishes,

Craving the happiness of this life alone, without any other
aspiration, makes us ultimately no different from an animal.
If, like an animal, we seek nothing but pleasure of the material
body, it is extremely disappointing.

As human beings—with a precious human life with leisure and
endowments—we have the intelligence to transform our mind in
accordance with the Dharma. The Tibetan term *chö rabtu nampar
chepa*, "discernment of phenomena," has a vast meaning, as it is our
mind's capacity to discern—or to know via special insight (*vipashyana*)—the nature of all phenomena within samsara and nirvana. To
make our human life meaningful, it is important for us to use our discernment and turn our intelligence toward a positive direction. The
Kadampa master Puchungwa reminds us,

> Having attained the precious human life of leisure and endow-
> ments, dying without having created virtue is like throwing
> away a precious jewel we have found without using it!

We have been fortunate enough to be born in a place where the teachings of the Buddhadharma are known and we have the capacity to
hear and understand the teachings. If we do not have the capacity
to learn the teachings, then it is impossible to practice the Dharma.
The great teacher Longchenpa reminds us that being born as a human
being is a unique and rare situation—we are like a blind person who
accidentally found a precious jewel. Similarly, we have found a human
birth and we need to realize how fortunate we are.

There are approximately seven billion people on this planet. Of
these, only five hundred million might be Buddhists, and those who
practice the Dharma are fewer. Many people say that they are Buddhist, but they do not practice and meditate. Thinking about this,
you can understand why the Buddha said that the number of virtuous

people in the world is only the amount of sand that can fit on your fingernail. In contrast, those who are not virtuous are as countless as the sand in the oceans.

If we practice the Dharma correctly, we will find peace and happiness and attain liberation. Furthermore, if we practice and accomplish virtue, then the latter part of our life will be happier than the earlier part, and our next life will be happier than this life. We will experience increasing amounts of happiness. On the other hand, if we don't use the precious opportunity to practice in this life, we will remain in samsara. By focusing only on accomplishing worldly aims or performing negative actions, we will suffer more in the latter part of this life than in the earlier part, and we will suffer worse in our next life than in this life. It is up to us.

The Buddha observed and advised his students to understand what we have done in the past and where we are going to be born next by looking at what we are doing now. To see where we are going to be born next, we should look at what we are doing now. Similarly, Padmasambhava teaches that if we want to know our past life, we should look into our present condition; if we want to know our future life, we should look at our present actions.

Please understand the value of your precious human life. This will give you the opportunity to practice *lojong* (mind training). By training your mind you will understand who you are and your life will be meaningful. If you are deceived into perceiving this pleasant life's appearances as permanent, you will fall under the influence of deluded states of mind and experience continual suffering. You must ensure that you do not create your own suffering.

Why do we worry so pointlessly about our temporary happiness? If we have the power to benefit others, why not put effort into it? The Buddha taught that life in this world is unsatisfactory, as it doesn't offer unchanging, permanent happiness, harmony, and comfort. We cannot pass beyond this pervasive suffering while we are in the world because our mind is blinded by desire and constantly unsatisfied.

Therefore, it is important for us to practice what we have learned from our meditation. Practicing meditation on such topics as patience, tolerance, impermanence, love, compassion, and the over-all preciousness of human life can help us to overcome the causes of suffering and teach us how to live meaningful lives on the path to enlightenment. Human beings have great potential that can be real-ized. Each one of us is capable of experiencing joy, love, clarity, and openness. These experiences are our true nature—our liberation from suffering.

Happiness in Life

To have a happy life, we need a healthy body and mind and suitable living conditions supported by a good livelihood. In addition, if we want a meaningful life, then we need an authentic spiritual path. All of these make life peaceful, happy, and enjoyable. Together, they allow all our actions to become the cause of enlightenment and happiness for ourselves and others. Our relationship with life and work is based on our state of mind and how we relate to others. If we wish to man-age our life, we need to be mindful of the present moment no matter if we are at work or practicing meditation. Many people feel a sepa-ration between their spiritual and work lives. Some people who have developed renunciation may feel like they are wasting their precious life by working instead of practicing.

To change those feelings, it is important to do three things. First, you should try to correct your *motivation* at the beginning of your day, before your work begins. Second, try to practice *mindfulness* throughout the day, if you can. Third, try to *dedicate* all your work at the end of the day. If you do these three things, then you are not wast-ing your time—even if you feel a separation between your spiritual and work lives.

In thinking about happiness in life, we need to identify first the correct definition of happiness. Genuine happiness is quite unconnected to material things. Material things bring us temporary happiness, but they don't bring us genuine happiness. Teachers say that if your happiness relies on material things, then your happiness is of poor quality because it doesn't truly satisfy you and free you from desire and attachment. There are two types of happiness: relative happiness is the practice of satisfaction; ultimate happiness is a deep understanding of the nature of life. From my own experiences I know that happiness can only come from initially training the mind to practice contentment.

Usually we want to get rid of negative circumstances, which often means we try to ignore them. However, negative things are not always bad. Sometimes encountering negative situations can be a blessing; like a great teacher, the negative situation can wake us up from our ignorance. If we take every situation in life—whether positive or negative—as an opportunity to awaken our bodhichitta and compassion, then we are never separate from our spiritual life. As our capacity grows, we will be able to accomplish all our activities, and these activities will become more beneficial than before.

Remember that your work can help you develop discipline. Discipline means being able to recognize what is happening and knowing the right conduct for that situation—which may be doing something good for yourself or for others. Therefore, your work and home lives are excellent environments in which to develop your discipline—places where you can develop your motivation, good conduct, and mindfulness. Mindfully work, eat, talk, and so on, so that you can be aware of everything that is happening, without being caught in the past or carried away by worries about the future. If you take good care of the present, then there is no need to worry about the future.

If you are always worried about what others think about you, you will not enjoy your life. Whatever you do, people will always have something to say about it—you cannot control what others think, say, or do. However, it doesn't matter. What matters is having a good motivation that does not depend on others' thoughts at all. If you have a good motivation, then it doesn't matter what other people say or think about you. When you enjoy working and living life with a good motivation and mindfulness, you will be a creative and helpful person.

Letting Go of Stress and Anxiety

The main problem in life is often stress and anxiety itself, as these two distract us from our relaxed, natural state. How can we let go of stress and anxiety? What is the antidote? Our experience of anxiety and stress is directly related to our thoughts, our emotions, and the perceptions that we create in each moment. So how can we make a perfect relationship between our spiritual and work lives? When you know how to take care of your strong emotions and establish good relationships at work, communication improves, stress is reduced, and your work becomes much more pleasant. This is a great benefit not only for yourself but also for those with whom you work and live. As your knowledge of how to handle different situations grows, you will have more confidence in your ability to deal with your work and home lives.

My sincere advice is that you wake up with a great motivation and go to bed feeling content and satisfied. This will help you let go of your anxiety and stress. You need a good balance: if you try to bring your awareness to every moment—if you try to practice mindfulness in everything you do—your work can help you realize your ideal of living in harmony with others. However, working without these practices cannot give you such happiness. Practicing mindfulness is learning to relax and focus your attention on the present moment to enjoy the beauty and vitality of life—no matter how that energy manifests in your various life situations. Your life *as it is* presents you with all types of opportunities to practice.

Mindfulness helps you to be fully present. You can learn to handle your stress and anxiety by bringing relaxation into your life and by keeping yourself in the present moment. If you practice mindfulness, leave whatever strong emotions arise alone, and they will naturally dissolve into the nature of mind.

Practicing this art of letting go, you will experience increased joy and peace. You may think mindfulness is something that you can only practice when you have time. That is not true. You can practice mindfulness anywhere, anytime—even during a busy day at work. Simply try to let go of thoughts about the past and future by staying in the present moment. Open your mind and generate awareness of your natural peacefulness and joy.

If you practice mindfulness in your daily actions, then you will reduce stress by enjoying your life more. Many of my spiritual friends work very hard and have challenging times with their coworkers. They often ask me for advice on how to improve their daily work situation. I advise them to practice mindfulness combined with bodhichitta. Once they take care of their own mind, the same situations at work don't bother them in the same way because they have established peacefulness within their own mind. Therefore, outer circumstances do not stress them in the same way as they previously did.

Your work can be a wonderful method for you to express your deepest aspirations; and it can be a source of great peace, joy, happiness, and generosity. Conversely, the work you do and the way you do it may cause a lot of suffering. If you practice mindfulness, it does not matter how much you work—as long as you try to mix your practice with all of your activities, you can do everything in a suitable way that accords with the Dharma.

The ultimate goal in mindfulness practice is not just relaxation. It is about paying attention with sensitivity. One breath taken mindfully can change your relationship to your experience in that moment.

Therefore, try to practice mindfulness during your daily activities. Mindfulness practice establishes attention in the present moment. This practice gives you the best ability to concentrate your mind and helps you to find the best connection to yourself, your work, and your entire life. If you don't have this practice, then you will be anxious and feel that you are wasting your precious life. When you are having a hard time, remember impermanence. Every situation is temporary—your emotions, feelings, and thoughts will change. Nothing is permanent. Therefore, don't be stressed or have anxiety, because no matter how bad your situation is, it will change. When you face worrisome situations, remember this helpful advice from Shantideva's *Bodhicharyavatara*:

> So come what may, I'll not upset
> my cheerful happiness of mind.
> Dejection never brings me what I want;
> my virtue will be warped and marred by it.
>
> If there's a remedy when trouble strikes,
> what reason is there for dejection?
> And if there is no help for it,
> what use is there in being glum?

Good Conduct

How can you avoid harming others and practice good conduct? First, when you go to work or do any type of activity, as I mentioned above, your *motivation* is very important, as it is a method to transform everything into the kind mind of bodhichitta. Second, your *commitment* is important, as it is a method to improve your work and home lives. Third, your *conduct* is important, as it is a method to accomplish great benefit.

Conduct is the method to restrain yourself from degenerate, unsubdued actions and to maintain correct perception and proper action when relating to others. Good conduct can only come from training our mind and cultivating beneficial attitudes such as mindfulness, bodhichitta, and wisdom. In brief, correct conduct is to be honest and upstanding in our relationships and to refrain from harm and provide assistance when we are able. We can become powerfully effective people in dependence upon perfect conduct; without it, it is impossible to help others effectively. Therefore, it is important to conduct our life by abandoning activities that harm innocent beings for the sake of protecting and supporting one person—namely, our *selfish self*—and to practice a truthful path of honesty and upstanding behavior. Good conduct reflects our respect for the preciousness of ourselves and others. By respecting and benefiting others, we benefit ourselves.

We usually have a wrong view and think of benefiting ourselves rather than others. Take a moment to examine whether you feel that if you benefit others, you will lose something. If you have this attitude, consider changing it by seeing if good things come back to you when you help others. Great teachers tell us that this is the law of nature. By understanding this, you will be able to work and live peacefully with others. All your life situations involve clear communication and honesty. If you do your work sincerely and live an honest life, then even if something goes wrong, you won't have regrets and you will be content and satisfied with your life. Be mindful of this precious moment. Remember how short your life may be—being mindful of impermanence will help you focus on practicing the good conduct of bodhichitta that is beneficial to all living beings. To summarize,

> That supreme guide who loves all as his children taught
> bodhichitta motivation as foremost of all.

Those who have it can accomplish all.
Those who lack it are unfortunate.
What else differentiates virtue and vice?

4

Renunciation

If you are a Hinayana practitioner, you must have a mind of renunciation, seeking to rise above and abandon samsaric existence. If you are a Mahayana practitioner, you must also have the precious mind of bodhichitta, seeking to benefit others. To awaken our buddha nature, we should train in these two aspects of the teachings—renunciation and precious bodhichitta. Without at least one of these, we cannot undertake a complete practice of the Buddhadharma. Just as we must enter a building on the ground floor, we must begin our practice with a correct understanding of what the Dharma is and how to practice it correctly by stages.

As for the mind of renunciation, day and night we must strive to diminish our attachment to this life and aspire to liberation. It is written in *Parting from the Four Attachments*:

Attached to this life, you are not a Dharma practitioner.
Attached to samsara, you have no renunciation.

Genuine renunciation is wanting liberation from samsara. Renunciation has two perspectives. First, with such an attitude, we look down at the suffering of samsara with no interest in it, and we wish to be completely free from suffering. Second, we look up at liberation and understand the benefit of liberation, and we wish to attain it. Some people are afraid that if they practice renunciation they will lose their pleasure and happiness in life.

In Tibetan the word for *renunciation* literally means "definite emergence" or "definitely going." Where must we definitely go? We must take the path of liberation. It is an attitude that aspires to liberation day and night. It can be practiced even while we are engaged in our daily life. In fact, sometimes we must practice a mixture of the Buddhadharma and our worldly work. As Khenchen Tsultrim Lodrö comments,

> The Mahayana teachings are for benefiting sentient beings.
> If we remain as divorced as earth and sky from all affairs that
> concern the welfare of sentient beings, how shall we accomplish the benefit and happiness of beings? Called a *vehicle of worldly gods and humans*, the Mahayana is a vehicle, or way,
> for gods and humans to experience happiness; how could it be
> something in which all connection with the world is completely unsuitable?

Without worldly people, how could practitioners of the Dharma survive by themselves? How, then, should practitioners and worldly people coexist? The Dharma is for the direct and indirect benefit and happiness of all living beings. Without sentient beings, there is no need for the Dharma. To paraphrase the words of Mahatma Gandhi,

> Temporal affairs separate from the spiritual are completely
> meaningless. First, we must make ourselves spiritually mindful

and introspective. As soon as we do that, we will discern the virtuous course in human affairs. That is the sacred right of all.

Therefore, it is not contradictory to engage in both the spiritual and the worldly; the worldly should support the spiritual and should be transformed thereby into the spiritual. Again, for the well-being of all sentient beings, in general, spiritual and worldly work must be pursued side by side.

You might think that if we don't give up this life and develop renunciation in our mind, that if we remain attached to the things of this life, we are not practitioners of the Dharma. It is true that there is a great danger that we will become attached and fooled into making insignificant matters of this life our sole concern. No matter how much wealth we have, we will not be able to bring the slightest portion of it with us on the day of our death. We must even part from this body that we have cherished so intensely. What goes with us and helps us at that time is the meritorious power of the good karma that we have created during our life. This is what helps and protects us.

Even if we cannot devote our entire life to our Dharma practice, it is extremely important to keep liberation as our principal ultimate aspiration and intention. To do so, renunciation and bodhichitta must be developed in dependence upon three types of nonattachment. As Minling Terchen Gyurme Dorje comments,

> First, by considering how difficult it is to obtain a human life
> of leisure and endowments, and by contemplating its imperma-
> nence, we are freed from attachment to this life and develop a
> genuine aspiration for fortunate future rebirth. Second, by con-
> templating the suffering of samsara and the natural law of kar-
> mic cause and effect, we are freed from attachment to samsara
> and develop a real aspiration for the definite goodness of our
> own liberation. Third, by meditating on love, compassion, and

bodhichitta, we are freed from attachment to selfishness and develop a genuine wish to attain enlightenment for the benefit of others.

We should not become attached to the pleasures of this life alone. To develop renunciation, we must realize that samsara has no essence at all. You might not wish to believe that samsara is without essence—that it has the nature of suffering. You may think that this is unpleasant and question how it could be correct. However, reflect upon how our human life is impermanent and very changeable. The more you think about physical illness and mental stress—plus all the distractions of daily life—the more you realize that your life has no permanent essence. We can see that our own mind is changing daily if we really think about it.

It makes me think about a man who owned a restaurant in Nepal. He worked nonstop without a break. He was not able to enjoy his money while living and not able to accomplish much spiritually due to lack of time. He died without spiritual development or worldly enjoyment. I think of this story when I think of why samsara has no essence. If we do not think about the suffering of samsara, it creates serious obstacles for us, as it is a major cause for not developing the aspiration for liberation or enlightenment.

Accordingly, those who wish for liberation and sincerely aspire to practice the Dharma must not be attached to samsara and its alternating appearances of happiness and suffering; they must persevere in the essential activities of the Buddhadharma. As this is very meaningful, I request you to contemplate it sincerely without worry or stress. Patrul Rinpoche teaches in his oral instructions,

If we sincerely intend to practice the Dharma, we must give it our utmost every moment. It requires day-by-day commitment. We must never forget it on any occasion.

How Buddha Shakyamuni Developed Renunciation

Buddha Shakyamuni's entire life is a profound teaching for those who follow him. He was born as the prince Siddhartha Gautama in the garden of Lumbini, near Kapilavastu in the foothills of the Himalayas, as the son of King Shuddhodana and Queen Mayadevi of Shakya in the sixth century B.C.E. He started school at the age of seven and completed his education. At the age of seventeen, he married Queen Yashodhara.

One day, he saw four signs—birth, old age, sickness, and death—that indicated that the pursuit of worldly things was of the nature of suffering. He felt immeasurably sad at the lack of essence in samsara and its nature of suffering. As a result, he developed the wish to attain not only his own enlightenment but great enlightenment so as to free all beings from suffering.

Wishing that he could ultimately free his loved ones from suffering, he decided to leave the palace and his family. Although he petitioned his father to be allowed to go, the king would not give him permission. When he was twenty-nine, Siddhartha Gautama unequivocally abandoned his kingdom and went to a sacred stupa, a reliquary monument symbolizing the enlightened mind of the buddhas, where he shaved his head, thereby ordaining himself.

He spent six years practicing austerities before completing his practice of the Dharma. At thirty-five, he attained enlightenment, becoming the great friend of all living beings. This all-accomplishing teacher did not leave his family and kingdom because he was incapable of protecting them—he left them out of great love and compassion.

He saw the absence of essential meaning in samsaric existence and wanted to establish all in ultimate happiness. This attitude is called renunciation—definitely going toward liberation. We should understand that the cyclic existence of samsara is without essence and discard it, putting effort into the supreme Dharma alone. We must do this, following the example of the Buddha and the early Kadampa masters of Tibet.

While it may be difficult, the most important thing is not to spend our time only in worldly pursuits, such as seeking friends and avoiding enemies. Without falling to either of the two extremes of conduct, we must exert ourselves in the practice of the Buddhadharma that brings benefit in this and future lives—*this is very important.*

How to Develop Renunciation

Start by understanding the value of your meditation and your Dharma practice—this is the practice of generating a mind filled with renunciation. What causes obstacles and makes us unable to succeed in our renunciation practice? It is following our desire and attachment by not finding satisfaction and contentment within our mind. To practice satisfaction is to practice renunciation. When we develop renunciation mind, we learn how to have a happy life. To have a happy life, we need to know how to enjoy life. Buddhism doesn't deny or reject this. To enjoy life, we need money to support our basic needs and to have fun. Buddhism doesn't reject this either.

To enjoy life, we also need the Dharma—the knowledge of what is right and wrong, and how to conduct ourselves with discipline. To accomplish this, the Dharma provides us with many wisdom teachings that liberate us from the suffering caused by our ignorance. Joy and happiness, enough money and material support, Dharma teachings and our spiritual path, and the enlightenment that comes from wisdom—these four aspects are important for our lives as they bring genuine happiness.

This kind of genuine happiness can only come from training our mind and shaping our attitudes. It is important to understand the value of the Dharma, the preciousness of life, and the opportunity that we must practice now. During the time remaining in this life, we should practice renunciation by practicing contentment, bodhichitta by practicing loving-kindness, and wisdom by realizing the true nature of all phenomena. The combination of these three is our ultimate goal. If we practice these diligently, our lives will be beneficial to all beings, including ourselves. On the benefits of developing renunciation and bodhichitta, Shantideva writes,

This free and well-favored human form is difficult to obtain.
Now that we have the chance to realize the full human
     potential,
if we don't make good use of this opportunity,
how could we possibly expect to have such a chance again?

Those who put off the practice of the Buddhadharma by distracting themselves with nothing but the attractions of this life, not to mention those who lack even the slightest inclination to practice, have no renunciation. No matter how much samsaric work we accomplish before beginning our Dharma practice, we will never be satisfied. The more wealth we possess, the more our desire increases. No matter how much we enjoy samsaric pleasure, it cannot give us permanent happiness.

Moreover, as we continually enjoy it, our desire is never fulfilled— our appetite only increases—and this creates even greater obstacles and suffering. Therefore, it is important to think about how samsara is pervaded by the three types of suffering, which were explained earlier. Its pleasures are but a temporary imitation of happiness. Ultimately their nature is nothing but suffering. As Mipham Rinpoche states,

Never satisfied, no matter how much happiness is experienced; never renouncing samsara, no matter how terrible it becomes. Alas, this mind is the primary cause of suffering! Look at the nature of this deceptive mind!

Misconceptions about Renunciation

When some people hear about renunciation, they think that they will have to give up everything. That is a misunderstanding of renunciation. Renunciation means *giving up our desire and attachment*.

For example, I am attached to my iPhone. I could give it away, and it might appear that I am practicing renunciation. However, the question I need to ask myself is, "Do I have a mind filled with renunciation when I give it away? Have I diminished my attachment to it?" If my desire and attachment are still there, it doesn't really matter how much I give up my property or my belongings. If I don't remove the root of the tree of my attachment, it doesn't matter if I have temporarily cut off the branch of the tree; the tree will grow again. I will buy another iPhone.

If our mind is full of desire and attachment, it doesn't matter how much we give up superficial things. As long as we don't have a mind of renunciation, we will be dependent on our desire—and there will be no satisfaction in our mind. Following desire is in itself suffering, and this is a problem.

As with the example of my iPhone, it is not our property or material goods that bind us but our attachment to them. Not having satisfaction and contentment is the nature and definition of desire—that is the biggest suffering within samsara. That's why the early Kadampa masters say that as long as you have attachment, you don't have a renunciation mind. Omniscient Longchenpa says,

Worldly activities will not cease until you die.
Only when you stop will they cease.
This is the way of things.

For example, the eighty-four mahasiddhas, who were accomplished masters of meditation, had many different lifestyles. However, they were not bound by samsara because of their renunciation mind and their realization of the benefits of liberation. The definition of having a renunciation mind is constantly longing for liberation, turning the mind toward enlightenment, and taking the path toward them. As Tsongkhapa Lobzang Drakpa says,

[When] all day and night the intention seeking liberation
   arises,
at that time, you have developed renunciation.

In Tibetan, *kyoshe* means sadness about samsara. When we reflect upon suffering and unhappiness, then we experience sadness. Once we understand suffering, we want to have freedom from it. That is what we call *nyejong* in Tibetan, meaning renunciation or taking the path of liberation. This intention to seek liberation is the mind of renunciation. We can start by practicing the path of satisfaction—by limiting our desire. Doing so can help us find our true path, for example, by practicing meditation, not causing harm toward others, and maintaining our motivation to practice the Dharma daily.

When we speak about the suffering of samsara, we should know that there is nothing wrong with samsara itself. The problem is how we relate to it. By not recognizing the true nature of our mind, we don't relate correctly with the reality of life itself. As we are ordinary people, we don't have a skillful method for looking clearly at our negative emotions. Therefore, we see negative emotions as disturbing and experience their energy as destructive. That particular view is based on our ego's perception of our emotions. In fact, according to Dzogchen masters, our experience of samsaric suffering is just the expression of the ground that is the fundamental, primordial state—our absolute nature—that is perfect and always present.

That's why the great meditators report that there is nothing to regret about samsaric experiences as samsara itself is in the state of liberation.

In Buddhism, we examine the mind and its relationship to the appearances of the world. We observe the mind to experience the mind itself as it is. Our main problem, though, is that the Dzogchen view of reality doesn't fit with our ordinary experience. So, we disregard the great perfection of reality as it is.

The foundation of all higher trainings, such as Dzogchen, is the practice of the preliminaries. These are the common outer preliminaries—the four thoughts about precious human life, impermanence, cause and effect, and renunciation—and the uncommon inner preliminaries—taking refuge, generating bodhichitta, purifying with Vajrasattva, offering the mandala, and meditating on guru yoga. The great master Patrul Rinpoche taught that these preliminaries are more profound than the so-called main practice as they are the foundation of all of the Vajrayana practices.

When your practice misses the essence of the preliminaries, even though you wish to practice the higher teachings, you will not have fully accomplished the aim of the preliminaries, which is the generation of a full conviction in the Dharma. Therefore, it is very important for you to make a strong decision and heartfelt promise to practice them. To summarize:

There is no renunciation without abandonment of samsara.
Why do I not wish to meditate without anyone telling me to
    do so?
Renunciation and contentment with few desires
Is the right attitude to which I am committed.

5

Bodhichitta

From how to develop a renunciation mind, we turn now to how to develop the enlightened mind of bodhichitta. What is bodhichitta? Bodhichitta is a compassionate mind of pure altruism that, as it ripens, opens our mind to the fullness of reality. *Bodhi* in Sanskrit means "enlightened" or "awakened"; *chitta* means "mind" or "heart." As we open to the experience of bodhichitta, we understand who we are and that we have the ability to care for others and ourselves on a great, limitless scale. Therefore, bodhichitta means a profound "enlightened attitude" or "awakened heart."

Ordinary love and compassion are usually based on a limited motivation rooted in selfishness. For example, many people practice patience, generosity, discipline, and the other virtues only toward those whom they consider part of *mine*—*my* family, *my* friends, or *my* group. However, beyond this limited motivation is a genuine, great love and compassion called bodhichitta. With this compassionate mind, all good qualities, such as love, expand infinitely. This is the great value of living our daily lives with the practice of bodhichitta.

If we can concentrate our mind on this motivation even for a moment, the merit will never be exhausted until our complete enlightenment as a buddha. The sutras say that whoever has a big heart has bodhichitta and whoever has bodhichitta has buddhahood. If our bodhichitta is stable, we are a bodhisattva who is mentally engaged with helping others limitlessly. This is the real purpose and meaning of our life. As Shantideva states,

> After fully considering it for many eons,
> the buddhas saw just this as beneficial.

Bodhichitta makes our mind strong and courageous. However, many people do not know this truth; they listen to the Dharma only for the purpose of gaining temporary benefits. The power of bodhichitta is that it changes our self-centered mind so that we stop harming others and understand how to develop good relationships with them. It is the heart of Buddhist practice and the basis of our enlightenment.

Cultivating Bodhichitta

When we practice the compassionate mind of bodhichitta, we must start by doing analytical meditation, as follows. Correct your motivation by reflecting that all sentient beings are like you in wanting happiness and not wanting suffering—this is our shared nature. As reported by Patrul Rinpoche in *The Words of My Perfect Teacher*, Trungpa Zinachen asked Padampa Sangye for a complete instruction in a single sentence. Padampa Sangye replied,

> Whatever you want, others all want as much; so act on that!

It is living beings' nature to strive for their own happiness. Not only human beings but all beings—even bugs—want happiness. If we don't stop harming them, how can we develop a good heart? Some foolish people think that there is no fault in killing animals, but this is mistaken. My wish is that all sentient beings have equal rights and the freedom to practice a path that follows the natural law of karma. We know from our own direct perception and experience that as long as sentient beings have consciousness, they feel the pleasure and pain that are, respectively, the result of helpful and harmful actions.

Since we know what it feels like to suffer in body, speech, and mind, we can use our own body as an example. If we exchange places with others, putting ourselves in their shoes and imagining how that would feel, we can clearly understand how they suffer and how inappropriate it is to harm them. As the Buddha says, taking your own body as an example, do not bring harm to others. Knowing from our own feelings what we do and do not want, we can infer what others do and do not want. The times that we have harmed others with body, speech, and mind are innumerable. As Dodrupchen Jigme Tenpe Nyima comments in his text *Transforming Suffering and Happiness,*

> Whenever we are harmed by sentient beings or anything else, if we make a habit out of perceiving only the suffering, then when even the smallest problem comes up, it will cause enormous anguish in our mind.

For the sake of just a little happiness in this life, we ignore the plight of others and act in harmful ways toward them. We should make a promise from the depths of our heart that from now on, we will abandon such acts to the best of our ability. For example, many of my spiritual friends have decided to become vegan to prevent causing harm to animals and the environment.

Whatever suffering living beings experience, it is because of their previous negative karma—their mistakes in their conduct. Controlled by their ignorance and tormented by suffering, samsaric beings want happiness but do not know how to create its causes. They do not want suffering but do not know how to abandon its causes. Their wishes and their actions go in opposite directions.

In general, think how pitiful this is for all sentient beings, and then focus upon those who are tormented by suffering. Reflect on this and vow to yourself: *I must become able to lead them out of samsara's sea of suffering. For this purpose, I shall practice the sacred Dharma.* We must develop repeatedly in our mind a vast altruistic intention focused on benefiting others out of great compassion. As Khenchen Jigme Phuntsok says, we should abandon selfishness like poison.

If you are an advanced bodhisattva who is completely altruistic and unselfish, then even the four activities considered extremely unwholesome in the Hinayana tradition—killing, sexual misconduct, stealing, and lying—may be regarded as part of the Mahayana path. Yet how can we, with our endlessly self-seeking attitudes, uproot self-interest right at the start? As Patrul Rinpoche remarks,

It is gradually, gradually, by stages of action,
that we become a victorious one—not all at once!

Training ourselves in the good heart of bodhichitta by repeatedly familiarizing ourselves with it, we should promise to completely give up selfishness gradually over time. Giving up our self-cherishing attitudes means that we must change our inferior motivation and abandon harming others for the sake of our own comfort and happiness. We should adopt the superior motivation of bodhichitta and be aware of the suffering of others, striving to help them when we can.

To practice the good heart of bodhichitta, there is no need to become a Buddhist. If we practice bodhichitta, we will have a sincere, truthful, and kind heart that will help us to have a happy life. Moreover, bodhichitta makes us powerfully beneficial to ourselves and others, helping us to serve our community and society to our greatest capacity. As Patrul Rinpoche urges,

The path of the Buddha is fully complete, supreme bodhichitta. Therefore, persevere in this best of minds; you, too, will soon become a buddha!

If we have bodhichitta, it is a great virtue. Even our ordinary activities become methods for the attainment of buddhahood. Developing bodhichitta destroys immeasurable collections of negative karma. It makes us inseparable from the liberating Dharma and beneficial to others wherever we go. It keeps us in harmony with others and earns us the respect and praise of all.

Therefore, not treating this as something insignificant, we should, as Patrul Rinpoche says, make our practice—preparatory, main, and the concluding stages—complete with bodhichitta. The details can be learned from the teachings on mind training (*lojong*) and from Patrul Rinpoche's *The Words of My Perfect Teacher*.

If you wonder how you can benefit sentient beings, the Buddha says that the supreme benefit for beings is to enter the Dharma—for the minds of sentient beings to transform into the Dharma. The Buddha's teachings exist only to bring benefit to beings; therefore, it is important for us to benefit beings by means of the Buddhadharma. For those to whom we are closely connected, nothing is more beneficial than teaching them what to practice and what to abandon—as this is the essence of the Dharma. As the *Vajracchedikaprajnaparamitasutra* says,

Sons and daughters of the lineage! Compared to a benefactor filling the entire billion worlds with the seven kinds of precious jewels and giving it to someone, if they were to express just one four-line verse of the Dharma to that person, the hearing of it, even if they do not understand it, is of greater benefit.

All of the six transcendent perfections, the paramitas, are included in this practice—therefore, they are bodhichitta in action. Setting beings on the path is one of the thirty-seven factors of enlightenment, the enlightening activities of the buddhas. If we help someone to develop love, compassion, and bodhichitta, they will gradually reach the bodhisattva path of accumulation, putting them directly on the path to great enlightenment.

HOW TO PRACTICE BODHICHITTA

In the morning when you wake up, make a commitment that all your actions that day will benefit others. Vow to help others as much as possible and remember not to harm them. This is the way to develop your bodhichitta mind every day. Set your good motivation and be mindful of your thoughts and actions during the day.

When you notice negative thoughts arising in your mind, transform them. Bodhichitta is the only way to handle the inevitable problems that will arise. Everything can be transformed by bodhichitta because it is the antidote to our selfish motivation. Since everyone has problems based on selfishness, everyone should practice bodhichitta in the way the Buddha advises. For example, during the Buddha's time, there was a monk who sat last in a row of people to be served food. He was worried there would not be enough for him to eat, so he moved to the front to be served first. But when he did this, he realized he was being very selfish and felt regret. This situation helped him to develop his bodhichitta mind. Therefore, we can see that these problems are not inherently bad, as they provide the basis for developing ourselves as human beings and for making our lives meaningful through practicing bodhichitta. This is called the seven-point training in cause and effect for developing bodhichitta. In *A Guide to the Words of My Perfect Teacher*, Khenchen Ngawang Palzang teaches how to meditate on the kindness of our parents:

> First, they are kind to give us life. In the middle, they are kind to raise us. Finally, they are kind to show us the world and give us what we need.

In this essential guidebook, Khenchen Ngawang Palzang gives very extensive instructions for meditation on bodhichitta, following the method of training the mind in recognizing beings as our mother, remembering their kindness, wishing to return their kindness, and so on. We should practice these methods to develop our bodhichitta.

How do we develop the good heart of bodhichitta? The first method is to remember the kindness of all living beings. *The Seven Points of Mind Training* advises us to meditate on the great kindness of all. Sentient beings are the foundation of our practice. Without suffering sentient beings, there is no way to generate love and compassion, and therefore we cannot engage in these practices. Every happiness that we experience comes to us through the kindness of other sentient beings—it all depends upon them. That is why Shantideva asks us, why don't we show respect toward sentient beings in the same way we respect the Buddha? Why don't we take care of sentient beings in the same way that we take care of ourselves? Without sentient beings, we would never have the opportunity to practice bodhichitta. We should be thankful for all beings because enlightenment depends on them.

Even after attaining enlightenment, we will still need sentient beings. With all our wisdom, compassion, and ability to work skillfully with others, what would we do without sentient beings? For the one who wishes to attain enlightenment, the buddhas and sentient beings are equally kind. If you really understand how important it is to have a bodhichitta mind, you will also understand how important sentient beings are to you. For example, without experiencing someone who is angry with you, how could you learn to be patient? How could you realize the perfection of patience?

The second method to develop the good heart of bodhichitta is for those who believe in rebirth. To practice the latter, visualize your kindest parents or friends—those whom you find most dear and pleasant to think of—present before you. Contemplate that they have been your loving parents from beginningless lives up to the present. Remembering this, bodhichitta arises effortlessly.

When the Buddha went begging for alms with his disciples, an elderly woman cried out to the Buddha, "My son, my son!" The Buddha told Ananda and the other disciples that she had remembered being his mother for many lifetimes. If you believe in past and future lives, there is no sentient being who has not been your parent in this or in past lives. Being aware of this, bodhichitta is easy to develop; a desire to work on behalf of others arises in you effortlessly.

After understanding that all living beings have been your parents, the next step is to remember the kindness that they have shown you. Think to yourself, *After I was born, my parents protected me with loving-kindness when I was incapable of keeping myself alive. When I was unable to eat, they taught me to eat. When I didn't know how to walk, they taught me to walk. When I was unable to speak, they taught me to speak. They showed me extreme kindness. In short, they kept me from dying when I was a child.*

Then, remembering their extreme love and kindness, you must examine if they are experiencing happiness or suffering. But you cannot help them solely by remembering their kindness. If you realize that your former parents are suffering, you must do something to return their kindness. Therefore, meditate on the good heart of bodhichitta, wishing to return their kindness by means of the Buddhadharma. There are two ways to return their kindness mentally by practicing aspiration bodhichitta: you wish them to have happiness and its causes; and you do not harm them with your body, speech, and mind.

Then you practice developing your ability to cherish and love others with affectionate compassion and to apply the extraordinary attitude of pure altruism in all situations. Finally, you develop bodhichitta, the wish for enlightenment that promises to establish tormented sentient beings into the state of a buddha.

When we correct our motivation in this way, whatever virtue we create is sustained by our vast intention to benefit others. It is a motivation that has two aspirations. The first is the compassionate aspiration to benefit others, seeking to fulfill others' purposes by helping them to attain temporary happiness and ultimately enlightenment. Motivated by great compassion for all sentient beings, we are determined to free them from suffering and to endow them with happiness. The second aspiration is for generating wisdom focused on the attainment of full enlightenment. We may not have the ability to achieve the welfare of other sentient beings presently but we can aspire to it.

For example, if we see a person suffering under the weight of a heavy load and we compassionately wish that they did not have to carry it, this is the compassion focused on benefiting others. If we actually carry this load ourselves, thereby freeing them from the burden, this becomes a metaphor for the wisdom focused on full enlightenment—the extraordinary intention of pure altruism.

Once we develop the good heart of bodhichitta, we have reached the lesser level of the first of the five paths toward liberation—the path of accumulation. From then on, never separated from kind intentions and the altruism seeking to benefit others in all our lifetimes, we develop increasingly higher stages of the bodhisattva grounds (*bhumi*) that lead toward enlightenment.

Therefore, bodhichitta is the root of all realized qualities. All the extremely profound and vast teachings of the Mahayana—including view, meditation, and conduct—come from it and nowhere else. There can be no superior instruction, even if we were to meet the Buddha in person and receive his teachings. The Buddha endured many long periods of austerities; the ultimate goal and the result of his extensive training are the methods for developing the good heart of bodhichitta.

Bodhichitta, the root of the entire Dharma, is having a correct and perfect motivation and conduct in the world. Without relying upon bodhichitta, we cannot attain liberation by any other path. Without bodhichitta, even if we would practice many hundreds of hours, we would not be walking the path toward the full fruition of enlightenment. For this reason, the Mahayana path emphasizes generating bodhichitta from the beginning of our journey until the attainment of enlightenment. If we develop bodhichitta, every practice we do becomes a cause of liberation. That is why all Mahayana teachers instruct that it should be the essence of our practice. As Khunu Lama Tenzin Gyaltsen advises,

If one investigates to find the supreme method,
for accomplishing the aims of oneself and others,
it comes down to bodhichitta alone.
Being certain of this, develop it with joy.

The open heart of bodhichitta allows us to be gentle with ourselves and kind to others—that is the best way to create healthy relationships with our family, friends, and neighbors. Based on our spiritual practice of bodhichitta, our ability to express love attains its highest level. Practice it diligently.

As Shantideva says, if you were to churn the milk of the Buddha's teaching, bodhichitta would be the butter. Like the tasty butter that emerges when milk is churned, bodhichitta emerges with practice. So, it is essential that, if it is still undeveloped, we develop bodhichitta first. With this excellent intention of bodhichitta, whatever we do will be especially beneficial and powerful. A practitioner who cultivates bodhichitta, the essence of what is beneficial, can be a healing presence to others. The healing power of bodhichitta is illustrated by Atisha, who requested the great master Dromtönpa to blow on his hand to heal its pain. He thought that it would be beneficial and powerful because Dromtönpa had a good heart.

From my experience, I know that meditating on bodhichitta can have a profound effect, leaving us feeling more peaceful and open so that we can relate easily to others and the world around us. For example, in my country of Tibet, in previous years, many great masters were imprisoned due to the conflicts at that time. Despite this, they never lost their compassion for the prison guards and they displayed great kindness toward them.

In Buddhism, we believe that we need to cultivate merit and wisdom through our practice to attain enlightenment. Practices done with bodhichitta are more powerful than those done without. Whether we are reciting prayers and mantras, making offerings, or performing other activities meant to benefit ourselves and others, we should perform them with a bodhichitta mind. Khenchen Padma Tsewang, my first root teacher, gave his students this advice about the benefit of bodhichitta:

The special method to subdue your wild, out-of-control mind is solely the precious good heart of bodhichitta. Therefore, without looking outside—practice it within. If we develop bodhichitta, the root of the entire teachings, even slightly, it causes us to develop a special certainty in the Dharma, to remember the kindness of our guru, and to develop compassion for sentient beings. It causes us to gain effortless, spontaneous accomplishment of all good qualities of the paths and the stages.

I have received many profound instructions on meditation repeatedly from many great masters in Tibet. After receiving teachings, remembering my gurus' instructions without forgetting or discarding them, I made notes of all that I could remember. Yet the most profound of all the instructions that I received were those on how to meditate on bodhichitta.

When I received these profound instructions, the idea of not practicing them made me immeasurably sad. That spurred me to make a strong determination from the depths of my heart to do my best to help living beings by means of these instructions and to make this nectar of the Dharma my innermost practice. I hope you will always do your best to practice these profound instructions in every situation. This is my heartfelt request to you and all my students. To summarize:

Daring to discard self-interest
and adopting altruism by taking responsibility for others'
    suffering—
though I lacked these two, even a reflection of them
is better than the fabricated altruism I had before!

6

Love and Kindness

Love, kindness, and compassion are attitudes that dispel suffering for all sentient beings, no matter who they are or whether they have faith and conviction in the Buddha's teachings. In the moments when you show true love and kindness, everyone is your friend. You are able to see how good everyone is, and they see that you are very special. Therefore, who doesn't need loving-kindness meditation?

When you think of benefiting all living beings, it is a great intention—a very big wish. Longchenpa says that if you wish to not harm others, then cultivate love and kindness. If you have a commitment to not harm and to love and care for others, then the benefit and result of this practice will be that you receive love from others in return.

As explained before, all sentient beings are the same in wanting happiness and not wanting suffering. In this way, all sentient beings are equal, but they are ignorant of what to take up and what to abandon to achieve those aims. Instead, under the influence of their negative emotions, they only create the causes of suffering. Love exclusively for our own benefit is a love mixed with attachment and aversion; it is not impartial, great love.

Although we wish to abandon unwanted suffering, we are under the control of our delusions and negative karma, so we create causes for nothing but suffering. Obscured from the means of achieving happiness, we wander into endless cycles of samsaric suffering and lower realms of existence. As Shantideva reminds us,

> Although wishing to be rid of suffering,
> they run right toward it!
> Although they want happiness, out of ignorance
> they destroy it like the enemy of their happiness!

Out of ignorance—by engaging in actions that are opposite to our wishes—we destroy our happiness as if it were our enemy. Reflect upon how sad this situation is! Just as it doesn't help to have food unless you eat it, having love is not enough for sentient beings. We must decide without doubt to accomplish the welfare of beings.

Likewise, if we want a good harvest, just having seeds is not enough—we must plant them. Wishing for sentient beings to attain buddhahood is virtuous, but as best we can, we should put the activities of the bodhisattvas into practice in our own lives.

How to Develop Love and Kindness

To engage in the activities of the bodhisattvas, we should generate love and kindness through meditation. When we first meditate, it may be difficult to develop great love for all sentient beings. This can be achieved gradually. Begin by focusing on the people and animals to whom you feel the closest—your friends, parents, or pets. Meditate on the following three steps repeatedly until transformation occurs: (1) remember the kindness you have received from these people and animals; (2) wish to reciprocate their kindness; and (3) develop cherishing love and affectionate compassion with a pure altruistic intent.

Eventually you will feel a great determination to bring these beings happiness—and then to bring all beings happiness.

When meditating on love and compassion, the great masters instruct us to meditate repeatedly with the four factors of aspiration, prayer, commitment, and request. Each step has a different motivation that generates corresponding feelings.

First, meditate on love in connection with aspiration, with the thought: *How wonderful it would be if all sentient beings had happiness!* or *If only sentient beings could have happiness!* Second, meditate in connection with prayer when you wish: *May all sentient beings have happiness!* Third, meditate in connection with a commitment when you determine: *I will bring sentient beings to happiness!* Fourth, meditate in connection with a request when you make the appeal: *Buddhas and bodhisattvas, please grant your blessings for all beings to be happy!*

You should feel the presence of all the lineage masters right in front of you. Think about the buddhas and bodhisattvas and request that they help you work for the happiness of all living beings. This is how you meditate on love using these four steps. When you meditate on compassion and bodhichitta, go through these same four steps.

You must develop love and compassion step by step by placing the seeds of commitment in your mind each time you practice. If, after meditating for some time on love, your meditation narrows to only those close to you or becomes mixed with attachment, the remedy is to meditate on great equanimity, freeing yourself from bias. Recognizing that all living beings, including animals, only want happiness can help you to free yourself from any bias in your meditation.

When you practice meditation on love, your heart should be like space—vast and open. In summary, as Shantideva expresses it in his dedication chapter of the *Bodhicharyavatara*,

As long as space endures,
as long as sentient beings remain,

until then, may I too remain
and dispel the miseries of the world.

GUIDED MEDITATION ON LOVE

Love is wishing happiness for ourselves and others. Sit comfortably with your back straight and your shoulders relaxed. Rest your attention on your breath. Think about impermanence—everything is changing moment by moment. Your life, the environment, and all outer and inner situations are all changing. When you breathe in and out, you should recognize that everything is changing. Therefore, this very moment is precious.

Recognize this and make a commitment to yourself by thinking, *I will be kind today. I am grateful for this moment. This moment is the best gift and very precious. I will love myself and others today. I am so grateful for all the good people in my life. I am so grateful for both good and bad times, as they have helped me to grow stronger. I will make a choice to be happy today. I am not going to let anyone or anything bring me down. Good things are coming into my life as I make these positive aspirations.*

Now, start to meditate, thinking, *May I and others be healthy, happy, and at peace.* Feel your love and generate happiness. Breathe in and out. When you experience inner peace between your breaths, focus in a relaxed way on that. Alternate between wishing yourself and others happiness—and resting in the gentleness of this meditation on love. When you have been doing contemplative meditation like this and your mind becomes tired, rest your mind for a little while. Don't chase after thoughts or think of anything; just remain in your natural state as best you can. As a result of practicing this meditation in alternation with resting meditation, you may feel gentler, kinder, and more peaceful.

7

Compassion

The Buddha said that wherever there is the sky, and throughout the space beyond, there are sentient beings. Wherever sentient beings are, there are also afflictions and karma. Wherever there are afflictions and karma, there is suffering. Therefore, if we sincerely wish for all sentient beings to have happiness, it is very important to practice compassion. As Chandrakirti says in his *Madhyamakavatara*,

> Compassion is the seed of this abundant harvest of liberation.
> It is like the water that causes growth and expansion,
> and it ripens into the state of lasting enjoyment;
> therefore at the outset I shall praise compassion!

To develop all the qualities of the Buddha's teachings, compassion is essential. Just as a seed is necessary for planting, as water is vital for growth, and as sunshine is required for fruit to ripen—if these three are complete, a perfect harvest will be enjoyed. Similarly, to develop all relative and ultimate qualities of realization, compassion is important at the beginning, middle, and end. Great compassion—like a seed—must be present for attaining the enlightenment that is the result of the bodhisattva path of Mahayana Buddhism.

The precious heart of enlightenment, bodhichitta, is this most necessary seed of great compassion. Therefore, it is important at the beginning. If we familiarize our mind with great compassion, it will be the source from which we develop all positive qualities—our compassion for others, our confident faith in the Dharma, our wisdom realizing emptiness, and our aspiration to attain full enlightenment. Therefore, compassion—like water for growth—is important in the middle.

Finally, all the buddhas' constant courageous efforts to benefit sentient beings depend upon great compassion—for example, by turning the wheel of the Dharma by giving teachings, by not abandoning sentient beings but cherishing them, and so on. Any act of body, speech, or mind that we undertake with compassion benefits ourselves and others. We're personally the first to benefit from the practice of compassion. Many of my spiritual friends tell me that they have less fear when they practice compassion because everyone starts to slowly appear to them as friends instead of enemies. This helps them to feel safer, more relaxed, less paranoid, and more at home in this world.

Therefore, compassion—like sunshine that ripens the fruit—is the final condition that enables the resultant harvest to be enjoyed. What we as Dharma practitioners aspire to is the loving, compassionate heart of enlightenment that is bodhichitta, which is the root of the Mahayana path. Thus, compassion is like the seed from which all the teachings grow and flourish.

If we can develop such compassion in our mind, it is fine even if we cannot do any other practice. As Buddha Shakyamuni states in the *Compendium of Dharma Sutra,*

O Bhagavan, a bodhisattva should not train in many
practices.

O Bhagavan, if a bodhisattva keeps to one practice and learns
it perfectly, he has all the Buddha's teachings in the palm
of his hand.

What is that one practice? It is great compassion.

The Three Types of Compassion

There are three types of compassion. The first is compassion that is
focused on sentient beings. Without discriminating among types of
beings—such as humans, animals, or other living beings—we practice
great compassion equally for all. According to the Buddha, to develop
compassion, it is important to consider all beings' situations equally.
We need to understand the suffering of others. As good practitioners,
we want to connect to all living beings—not just those to whom we
have a connection.

With the second type of compassion, we widen our compassion to
include not only sentient beings but all phenomena. There are two reasons for this. The first reason is that the Buddha says that we must treat
everything equally—not only all beings but all the elements as well. For
example, without the five elements (earth, water, fire, air/wind, space)
that appear to us as water, trees, soil, and other things, there is no life.
Therefore, we must take care of all phenomena equally. If these elements
are not healthy, then the environment will not be healthy—and everyone will suffer and become sick. The second reason is that everything is
impermanent. When we develop compassion by focusing on the impermanence of all phenomena, we will know how to deal with all types of
suffering. This focus helps us to change our fixation on all things being
permanent, and it lessens our desires by helping us to practice contentment and renunciation. To develop this second type of compassion, it is
crucial to understand the impermanent nature of all phenomena.

The third type of compassion focuses on reality, which is
beyond conception. The nature of everything is inseparable from

this great compassion. This compassion recognizes that all sentient beings possess buddha nature—the basic goodness that is the nature of mind. This is nondual compassion, the boundless nature of all phenomena.

GUIDED MEDITATION ON COMPASSION

When we meditate on love, we focus on generating the positive aspiration of wishing ourselves and others increased happiness. When we meditate on compassion, we focus on recognizing suffering and wishing to remove it. This may feel negative, sad, or uncomfortable at times, but the result of our meditation on compassion will be very beneficial. When we meditate, our object of compassion should be a specific person or animal; do not visualize the suffering of all beings.

Sit comfortably, close your eyes, and let your breath be natural. Think about a specific being who is experiencing great suffering. This could be an animal who is about to be butchered for its meat, for example. Visualize yourself in the place of this animal who will be slaughtered or another suffering being.

Once, I witnessed two people killing a rabbit. One person grabbed the rabbit and gave it to the next person to slaughter. First, he chopped off the rabbit's head. Then he chopped off all four legs and the tail. Then there was just the center of the body, but it was still moving. Visualize yourself as that rabbit. How do you feel? If you do this meditation, visualizing yourself as another suffering being will help you understand how that suffering feels. By practicing like this, you can develop your compassion and train yourself to see all beings as equal. It will undermine your desire to harm other living beings.

As you continue to practice compassion in this way, it will become more tangible and real. Then you can begin to expand your practice to encompass more beings with a strong feeling of concern and compassion. When you see the suffering of others directly in front of you, then you will be able to generate compassion and bodhichitta easily. Make the aspiration to develop bodhichitta in your heart to benefit sentient beings.

Our mind can do anything—good or bad—when it becomes accustomed to it. There will be times when you feel that your meditation practice on compassion is difficult or of no use. It is natural that such obstacles arise for those new to the practice. But if you persevere without discouragement, you will become compassionate like the Buddha.

As pointed out earlier, when meditating on compassion, put yourself in the place of suffering beings by exchanging yourself with others. Ask yourself, *If such suffering were happening to me, could I bear it?* If you could not bear it, why should another sentient being be able to bear it? Your compassion should be so strong that you genuinely wish that you could free them in that very instant. If you vividly meditate with such intense compassion, tears will naturally come to your eyes.

As a beginner, you have not trained your mind, so it is difficult to have love and compassion for all sentient beings without preference or bias. As explained earlier, begin by meditating upon those whom you naturally like, such as your friends or your parents. Continually expand your practice of love and compassion to include strangers, those who harm you, and finally all sentient beings—thinking how wonderful it would be if they could all have happiness and be free of suffering.

The Difference between Love and Compassion

The attitudes of love and compassion, respectively, are the wish for all sentient beings to have the happiness that they lack and to not be parted from the happiness that they have; and the wish for all sentient beings to be free from suffering and to not meet with more suffering.

The essence of love is an attitude that wishes and intends: *As sentient beings lack happiness, how wonderful it would be if they could be happy! I will bring them to happiness!* This gentleness is the essence of the practice of love. This love is like a mother bird taking care of her chicks. Chandrakirti teaches us that achieving benefit for all living beings is what is called *great love*.

The essence of compassion is an attitude that wishes: *If only sentient beings could be free of suffering! I shall free them from suffering!* Chandrakirti says that fully protecting those who are suffering is what is called *great compassion*.

Mahatma Gandhi suggests,

We see the power of love and compassion between parents, children, siblings, and friends, but we must practice spreading it to all sentient beings.

As he explains, love and compassion must be extended to all beings— not just those to whom we are partial. The root of Mahayana Buddhism is an attitude that greatly cherishes other living beings. If we take good care of a field, we will grow good crops. Similarly, from cherishing other sentient beings we attain the state of a buddha, completely fulfilling the needs of ourselves and others. When we have hatred or envy, or when we hold grudges, we see others as unpleasant or repulsive. When we have love and compassion, we view others as beautiful and loving. The attitudes of love and hate are opposites.

Their modes of apprehension are directly contradictory. Therefore, the more we meditate on love and compassion for someone, the more our hatred or uncaring attitude toward them diminishes. The more our dislike or hatred for someone grows, the less we will want them to be happy or to have good fortune.

In particular, if we lack altruism and a correct view of the world, our actions will lack meaning and our life will be wasted. Similarly, communities lacking love and compassion will be filled with conflict and war, robbing and plundering, and the killing of innocent people and animals—all of which ruins those communities and destroys others as bad conduct increases and good, noble conduct declines.

The Buddha said that we must protect everyone with loving-kindness and treat everyone equally. Love, kindness, and compassion benefit ourselves and others. When we have a deep understanding of the suffering of others, we will naturally wish for all beings to have freedom from suffering without discriminating between them. Unfortunately we often discriminate based on socioeconomic circumstances, race, gender, religion, species, and so forth. We know that we all wish to have happiness, yet we must reflect deeply upon the suffering of others in order to develop boundless compassion.

When we are jealous, competitive, or disparaging of others, our life will be filled with nothing but fear and frustration—what could be sadder than that? Therefore, the best source for peace and happiness in our world is loving-kindness and compassion. It is very important to train in these attitudes at all times.

Whether we are a worldly being seeking only the happiness of this life or a Dharma practitioner aspiring to benefit our future lives, we want to be a good person. Needless to say, on this earth that we all share like members of one family, if we can keep good, honest intentions and not deceive one another, and if we help others and renounce harming them—if we can truly practice love, compassion, and bodhichitta—everyone will enjoy happy lives. As a sutra states,

Wherever there is a head, there is life.
Wherever there is compassion, there is bodhichitta.
Wherever there is bodhichitta, there is buddhahood.

Self-Hatred and Self-Kindness

What makes self-hatred arise? While I am not certain about the causes of self-hatred, I do know that many people are struggling with it. Some people think that there is something wrong with them— something that cannot be fixed. However, you can change your self-hatred and transform all your negative emotions into positive ones. To develop your self-kindness, you need acceptance, because acceptance is the essence of spiritual practice and self-love.

Try to accept your body as it is, your mind as it is, and your emotions as they are—try to accept everything about yourself and practice self-kindness. If you can accept everything, then you can change. If you accept yourself with self-love and self-kindness, that is the solution to self-hatred. To look down upon yourself destroys your ability to increase your love for yourself and others because loving and accepting yourself is the essence of your courage to connect with yourself and others.

You might not like your actions, but to improve them you must first accept them. For example, some of my spiritual friends don't really like themselves, and they practice self-hatred. I often advise them to acknowledge and recognize this as the first step toward developing more self-kindness. (See the teachings on self-hatred on my YouTube channel.)

Try to stay realistic and not believe the meaningless reasons that your dualistic mind offers to you that makes your life miserable. Never think that there is no solution to your problems. With an open mind, look for solutions—then connect with the right situation, right person, right time, and right methods to help yourself. By being open to making these powerful connections, you can feel confident that you can do whatever it takes to solve your lingering problems and obstacles.

It is true that you will never be a perfect person if you don't purify your negative karma by changing your actions. And if you never stop accumulating negative karma, you will never feel good about yourself as a person. But you can stop accumulating negative karma now—and you can transform yourself. Your natural innate qualities—love, compassion, forgiveness, patience, bodhichitta, wisdom, and your buddha nature—are all perfect human qualities that you already possess. If you practice these, they will help you diminish your self-hatred and feelings of imperfection. These practices, which I will share, help you relax and move gently toward self-love—because you are making the connection between you and your qualities.

You must connect especially with your buddha nature, as this is the thing that makes you a perfect person. That's why, from the Buddhist point of view, you are not an evil person; rather, you are primordially and naturally a pure and perfect person. You might ask, how can we know that our nature is pure and good when we don't see ourselves that way? We are like a window with dirt; our unclear view obscures our potential. However, that unclear view is superficially on the window; the dirt is not the window's nature. As we clean the window, we will see more and more of the pure and clear view.

Our mind is just like the window. It's not intrinsically stained. As we practice, we will reveal more and more of our basic goodness, our natural purity. Don't ever think that there is something intrinsically wrong with you. Your nature is pure and radiant. As our inner discovery of these qualities progresses through meditation practice, the state of our inner life improves. Inner harmony, clarity, and stability come about. As we become more generous and loving, leaving the confused, ignorant mind behind, our life becomes happier and more open. That is true liberation—the self-love and self-kindness that results from meditation.

GUIDED MEDITATION ON FORGIVENESS

To change your self-hatred and develop your self-kindness, you should meditate on forgiveness. To practice forgiveness meditation, sit comfortably. Rest your attention on your breath for a few moments, relaxing as you breathe in and out. Let your body and mind relax. Let whatever emotions arise come and go. When you are ready, bring to mind a situation in which you have caused harm to yourself. Recall something that you feel bad about because of your actions, behavior, emotions, or your way of thinking.

Ask yourself, *How does it make me feel about myself? How does it prevent me from being happy? Why does it seem unacceptable and unforgivable?* Allow yourself to feel your answers directly in your body and mind. Once you clearly understand the main cause that makes you dislike yourself, then offer forgiveness to yourself. You should start to offer yourself forgiveness toward whatever feelings, thoughts, and behaviors you are rejecting.

As you practice like that, you may feel as if you are merely going through the motions and are not actually capable of forgiving yourself. You might believe that you don't deserve to be forgiven. You might be afraid that if you forgive yourself, you will just do the same thing again. If these doubts and fears arise in your mind, you should accept them with self-love and self-kindness by forgiving yourself. Your intention to forgive is the seed of forgiveness.

You may say to yourself, *It is my intention to forgive myself when I am able.* Take a few moments and try to connect with yourself through this practice. Remember your basic goodness, then relax and open your heart. Then say these prayers for yourself:

May I accept myself just as I am. May I be happy. May I know the natural joy of being alive. May I feel my loving-kindness.

Let your self-love grow as you say these prayers of love. Hold yourself in your heart and recognize the preciousness of your life. Then just relax there. Allow yourself to rest in openness and awareness. To end your practice, say prayers for other living beings:

May all beings experience love and kindness. May all beings recognize their buddha nature. May there be peace everywhere.

8

Tonglen Practice: Giving and Taking to Awaken Compassion

The practice of *tonglen*—giving our happiness and taking others' suffering—has been taught by Atisha and many great meditation masters to cultivate bodhichitta. The purpose of tonglen practice is to develop your loving heart as well as your compassion. The practice begins with your aspiration to help others, including yourself, and then extends that aspiration to ever-increasing numbers of living beings. You start by understanding how to care for yourself and those whom you love. Then, with practice, you develop your bodhichitta over time and can increase your capacity to extend love and compassion to those beyond your family or friendship circle.

This meditation on love and compassion has two aspects: (1) we meditate that sentient beings experiencing extreme suffering are present before us; and (2) we practice sending them happiness and taking on their suffering on the basis of our breath. Geshe Chekawa says that giving and taking should be practiced alternately and that this alternation should be placed on the medium of the breath. With our inhalation, we take away suffering by means of great compassion. With our exhalation, we send out happiness by means of great love.

When you visualize suffering in this practice, what you visualize should appear very vivid and real. Likewise, the compassion and love that you feel should be heartfelt. If your tonglen meditation remains just an intellectual exercise, it will never touch your heart. If you do tonglen practice according to the instructions, the practice works—it will develop your kind heart, your capacity to genuinely care for others, and your bodhichitta mind. This is the goal of the practice. As Shantideva states,

> Even if we lack power to help others in action,
> we should always keep the intention to do it.
> One who has that intention
> will actually engage in it.

Even if we have such an intention, we may not be able to accomplish vast service for sentient beings. However, we will remain mentally engaged with the compassionate motivation of a bodhisattva, and that is beneficial in itself. As Mipham Rinpoche remarks,

> Even if we do not have the ability,
> it is the promise that wishes to do it.
> If we do not wish to give that up, even to the end of the eon,
> if our bodhichitta is stable, we are a mentally engaged
>   bodhisattva.

GUIDED TONGLEN PRACTICE

In my lineage, the great master Patrul Rinpoche and my root teachers repeatedly gave these instructions on tonglen from their own experience.

First, when you practice tonglen, sit quietly and correct your motivation. You should pray to all the buddhas, bodhisattvas, and enlightened beings from the depths of your heart so that through their blessings, love and compassion will manifest in your heart and this practice will benefit others and bring them happiness.

Second, visualize your breath as a white wind that leaves your nostrils and goes toward the sentient beings in front of you. The white wind symbolizes your life, merit, wealth, physical and mental happiness, and all virtues of the past, present, and future. These beneficial qualities are inhaled by the sentient beings; they pervade them and cause them to experience ultimate happiness and bliss. Meditate this way to train your mind in great love.

Third, visualize that the sentient beings in front of you exhale all their suffering as a black wind that you inhale. As it pervades you, it takes away all the causes of their sufferings, karma, and delusions, thereby removing all imprints that result in suffering. Meditate that they are thus freed of all physical and mental suffering through your exercise of great compassion. You should meditate in this way with anywhere from one to an infinite number of beings; although, for beginners, it often works best to start with one being.

Fourth, when you experience unwanted sickness or other hardships, meditate upon all the sentient beings in the world who have a similar type of suffering. From the depths of your heart think, *May their suffering ripen upon me and may they be freed from all suffering and endowed with happiness!* When you are feeling happy and blissful, think, *Through the merit of this happiness and virtue, may all sentient beings be endowed with bliss!*

When you practice tonglen, contemplate that you compassionately take on sentient beings' suffering through the black wind. Thereafter, take a long, slow inhalation and hold your breath briefly. Then with a gentle exhalation, contemplate that you lovingly send out your happiness and so forth, with the visualization of sentient beings receiving all your well-being as the white wind pervades them.

As you continue your practice and it becomes stabler, more real, and more heartfelt, expand your tonglen practice of giving and taking to include more and more sentient beings. This is how you develop your bodhichitta, love, and compassion. If you become tired when you practice, then simply do resting meditation—remaining as long as you can without thoughts—as part of your meditation on ultimate bodhichitta. Generating pure, selfless altruism may be difficult for a beginner, but it is important to continually train your mind by repeatedly familiarizing yourself with this.

Benefits of Tonglen Practice

You may wonder if you should practice tonglen because you fear losing your happiness by taking on others' suffering. You need not worry as tonglen meditation undertaken with precious bodhichitta is the root of all higher practices—the heart essence of all the Buddha's teachings. It is a powerful, virtuous practice that results only in happiness, never in suffering. Among the metaphors for bodhichitta, one that merits discussion is the shepherdlike way of arousing bodhichitta.

Shepherdlike bodhichitta is based on how shepherds and herders send their animals out to pasture and then follow them. The shepherdlike way of generating bodhichitta is to think, *Having first set all sentient beings on the path of liberation, I will then attain enlightenment.* You may have questions about the rationality of this type of bodhichitta, such as *If sentient beings are limitless, is it possible that all sentient beings could become buddhas, leaving no one in samsara? Even if it were possible, once all sentient beings became buddhas, what need would there be for anyone to become a buddha in the future? Who would buddhas benefit by turning the wheel of the Dharma? Is this shepherdlike bodhichitta sensible?*

The reason you train your mind by generating the shepherdlike bodhichitta when practicing tonglen is that, as a result, your wish to practice the Dharma will grow stronger, preventing you from becoming discouraged. It also shows how limitless and powerful the bodhisattva's aspiration prayers are. Likewise, the Buddha generated such vast and altruistic intentions, but the result was that he attained enlightenment first and then accomplished the benefit of sentient beings. As Shantideva states,

> Whatever happiness exists in the world arises as a result of altruism.
> Whatever suffering exists in the world arises as a result of selfishness.
> What need is there to say much? The childish seek their own benefit,
> while buddhas act for the sake of others. Look at the difference between the two!

Sentient beings have cherished themselves above all others from beginningless time—working for their own sake alone—with the result that they now suffer in samsara. Buddhas, on the other hand, have discarded self-interest—helping others exclusively—with the result that they have exhausted all faults and limitations, obtained all qualities, fulfilled the purpose of themselves and others, and become the true friends of living beings.

Sending your happiness and taking on others' suffering via tonglen has the power to increase the benefit of all your meditation practices and gives you more inner strength and confidence. It removes obstacles to gathering the accumulations; it purifies negativity, self-grasping, and ego; it increases all virtue, and transforms all activities into the path. In short, it is something that can accomplish your true purpose. There is no instruction that surpasses it. Enjoy it and persevere in your practice of it.

Patrul Rinpoche says that if we do not become familiar with tonglen through continual meditation, we cannot expect it to be suddenly effective when we meet difficult conditions, such as illness, when our self-grasping delusion becomes even stronger. Therefore, it is important that we practice tonglen regularly when our lives are going well. In the tradition of Atisha Dipamkara Shrijnana, we should not forget bodhichitta and tonglen meditation whether we are eating, lying down, walking, or sitting. It is something to meditate on continuously. As a result, our breath and mind gradually become unified so that our mind does not wander; we achieve shamatha with mindfulness and alertness, and we develop love and compassion. The measure of having successfully developed tonglen practice through love and compassion in your mind is the love and compassion felt by a parent without arms whose infant is carried off by a river. To see their beloved baby being swept away would cause them unbearable, intense suffering; but lacking arms, they cannot rescue their child. When you develop genuine love and compassion like that for all sentient beings—not abandoning them, always thinking about their suffering, and ignoring your own welfare for their sake—that is the full development of your bodhichitta mind.

To summarize:

Dzogchen meditation without bodhichitta and compassion
is not the Buddha's supreme path.
If we meditate on tonglen, pacifying selfishness,
freedom from deluded pleasure and pain is bliss.

9

Entering Shamatha Meditation

In previous times, after the Buddha's precious teachings had spread widely, many people manifested the results of the path and achieved enlightenment in one lifetime. In the *White Lotus of Compassion Sutra*, the Buddha says that present-day sentient beings like us would be extremely difficult to teach how to train our minds. Seeking only the things of this life, we mistakenly engage in strong negative thoughts and actions; meeting with all sorts of suffering and torment, we lack compassion. The Buddha says that during such times as these, regardless of training and effort, it would be difficult for people to immediately develop realizations of the profound view.

Therefore, it is important first to develop the practice of the meditative concentration of shamatha—in Tibetan, *shiné*—a deeply peaceful concentration or absorption in stillness, perhaps best translated as "calm-abiding meditation." Shamatha is a meditation in which the movement of the mind toward outer objects—forms, sounds, or other objects of the six senses—is calmed so that the mind dwells within, focused solely on its observed internal object, such as the breath.

The word *shamatha* can be broken down into *shama*, which means "peace"; and *tha*, which means "dwelling," "stability," or "abiding." This peacefulness means that the mind is not overcome with anger, sadness, craving, or any other strong emotion that might distract it from its object of meditation—such as the breath or a Buddha statue—on which it calmly abides. When resting in shamatha meditation, the mind is relaxed and at ease without difficulty. It is not involved in forced or contrived activity but naturally rests in a state of peaceful stability. As the mind rests single-pointedly on its object, it is not distracted by external objects. It remains stable and so focused on its object that few thoughts arise; the mind is calm. In short, *shamatha* means "peace."

The attainment of shamatha meditation allows a practitioner to enter any of a large number of meditative concentrations called *samadhi*. The Sanskrit word *samadhi* means "to hold things together"; the Tibetan equivalent, *ting nge dzin*, means "to hold things firmly without movement." In English, *samadhi* is often translated as "meditative concentration." According to Mipham Rinpoche, samadhi is a balanced mind that remains solely focused with its full capability on an object—abiding in balance, in accordance with its object, and tending neither toward sinking nor excitement.

Why must shamatha meditation be cultivated before vipashyana (insight meditation)? When calm abiding has been achieved, all subsequent analytical meditation and all virtuous activities will have great power as the mind is engaged without distraction. In addition, shamatha is the basis of other types of meditation, all of which require the clarity and stability gained from the foundational practice of calm-abiding meditation.

When practicing shamatha, a beginning meditator is not capable of remaining focused on their object for even a moment; they may even feel that their mind has more thoughts and is more excited or agitated than before. Noticing this is actually a sign of progress in meditation.

In either case, try not to be dejected, discouraged by laziness, or think that you cannot meditate. Often, my students think that shamatha meditation makes their thoughts more gross—more coarse, vivid, or exaggerated—but this is not true. Through their practice of meditation, they are simply becoming more aware of the energetic qualities of their thoughts, which they previously did not recognize.

Don't think that as a beginner you will be unable to meditate on the spiritual path. Through methods learned from your teacher's instructions, you will still your mind. If you can uplift your mind without stopping your meditation practice, eventually your coarse thoughts will be pacified so that you can remain focused on your object for a few moments or even longer. You need to apply many methods without trying too hard or becoming overly serious about it.

At first you cannot give the mind free rein to follow whatever thoughts arise, but you also shouldn't be too uptight about it. You must practice as suited to your nature and constitution. When the mind is concentrated too tightly, an increase of thought occurs, causing a dislike for meditation or even a serious disturbance of your heart energy. This is your subtle, inner wind energy and life force. Therefore, you must apply a suitable level of concentration and gently relax without pushing yourself to concentrate too much. At the same time, you should avoid allowing your concentration to get too loose.

My root teachers said that it is important to practice in frequent short sessions. With brief sessions, the mind is not obstructed by sinking or excitement, which I will explain shortly; and with frequent sessions, you develop genuine faultless meditation. Therefore, I advise beginners to meditate for no more than ten or fifteen minutes and to avoid pushing themselves too hard in their sessions.

When you practice meditative concentration, your thoughts may flow very strongly—like a stream rushing down a steep mountain— and it may be difficult for the mind to be still. At that time, you must not become discouraged. Remembering the beneficial qualities of meditative concentration, you should persevere by placing your mind on your meditational object repeatedly. If you do this, it is natural that you will make progress every day.

Because you have been long accustomed to following your thoughts without applying an antidote to mental wandering, it is not easy to bring the mind under control. However, as Shantideva remarks in the *Bodhicharyavatara*:

> There is nothing that does not grow light
> through habit and familiarity.
> Putting up with little cares
> I'll train myself to bear with great adversity!

If you practice with a suitable degree of focus and concentration—not too loose and not too tight—your mind, which is like a stream chasing after objects and turbulent with many thoughts, will attain more stability. Both coarse and subtle thoughts will become pacified. In this state of meditative concentration, you will feel joy naturally, and you will have enthusiasm for practicing. It is important to persevere in keeping the continuum of your meditative concentration steady. This feeling of naturally arising joy is the beginning of a samadhi that involves some movement of thought.

In this early phase of samadhi, the mind is like a mountain stream that has reached a constriction, where the water still moves without stopping, but it is calmer and more subdued than before. At this point, when directing the mind toward an object during meditation, there may sometimes be more clarity; the mind may be still at times and at other times, not. Under the influence of thoughts, the mind does not remain focused on a single point; it alternates between movement and stillness. It is important not to follow thoughts and to focus without fixation. Meditating like this continually, the muddy water of the mind, if left in stillness, will gradually be cleared of silt and all thoughts will be stilled. If you notice that your mind attains stability—focusing on your observed object without the interruption of thoughts—that is good.

How to Develop Shamatha Meditation

In *Stages of Meditation*, Kamalashila advises that the following conditions are helpful when practicing shamatha to develop meditative concentration:

> Stay in a conducive place where food, clothing, and so forth
> are easy to obtain, a place that is isolated and delightful;
> one must have few desires, be content,
> and completely abandon engaging in many activities.

As you practice, the development of your meditation follows three stages. The first stage, called having *one preparation*, involves preparing a solid ground for your meditation practice. This means that you should not expect any immediate results—don't expect enlightenment after one week or one month of practice. Prepare your mind for the obstacles that will arise during meditation. If your mind gets distracted when you meditate, do not worry, as this happens to all meditators. As soon as you become aware of distractions, just let them go and return to your practice.

If you don't lose your confidence when your meditation is going badly, the next time you meditate, it will be better. Just as when you drive you need to be confident that you will arrive at your destination, you need to be confident that you can overcome your habit of distraction and be able to handle anything that arises during your meditation session. Don't give up. Just keep practicing.

Your confidence comes from your view. The more confident you are of the view, the more confident you will be at every stage of the path. Before you meditate, prepare your mind by giving up hope and fear, as these give rise to all kinds of other emotions. Let go of your expectations for that session and simply meditate. For example, to give up expectations helps you overcome your hope for a good meditation experience and fear of a negative one.

The second stage requires two implements: *mindfulness* and *alert awareness*. Whether you have a good meditation or not depends on these two. Mindfulness and alert awareness are the essential tools you need for any kind of meditation. You cannot meditate without these two because you cannot hold your mind and the object together without them. How are you going to hold these two together? With mindfulness and alert awareness you can keep both in mind.

Mindfulness allows you to not forget what you are doing. By paying attention to the main focus of your meditation, mindfulness helps you focus on your object continuously. Your alert awareness helps you recognize distractions, such as thoughts or disturbing emotions. This is key because distraction is your main obstacle. Mindfulness keeps the mind in place, and alert awareness knows what is happening.

If, for example, your mind wanders during meditation, alert awareness makes you cognizant of the fact and you can refocus your mind on your object. With alert awareness, you will know what is happening. If your mind stays calm and relaxed, and if, at the same time, you notice some movement, then you have mindfulness and alert awareness. When your mind is calm, mindfulness is the *stillness of the mind*; alert awareness is *knowing that it is still*. Mind in this state has good energy and clarity, and this experience is very powerful. It comes from the ability of your mind to abide in the present moment.

The Three Qualities of Mindfulness

Teachers say that mindfulness has three qualities: *familiarity, not forgetting*, and *the ability to hold*. The first quality of mindfulness is *familiarity*. When the mind is able to remain with an object, it can understand what the object is. The more familiar you are with how your mind works, the stronger your mindfulness becomes. With familiarity you are able to recognize your thoughts, let them go, and return to the present moment.

In Buddhism, we talk repeatedly about view and meditation. Why? Think about it—what is your meditation? It is holding your mind to the view. The more you hold your mind to the view, the more you understand the view. And after a while, the view is not different from you; it is naturally who you are. It is the same with familiarity. For example, when you are meditating, your thoughts are taking place. What does *familiar* mean in this case? It means you are working with duality. When you become truly familiar, your dualistic thoughts dissolve and your mind relaxes.

After familiarity, the second quality of mindfulness is *not forgetting*. When you remember, you have mindfulness. If you are thinking about bodhichitta or emptiness all the time, then you are mindful of them continuously. Generally your experience in the first stage of meditation is the movement of the mind. If you have familiarity and not forgetting, then you have a continuous feeling of awareness that knows where your mind is.

The third quality of mindfulness is the *ability to hold* on to the object of meditation. When you focus on an object, it stays in your mind. The more you develop your meditation, the more your ability to hold the object in focus will increase. With less movement in your mind, your mind will become calmer and stabler. For example, when you first begin to meditate, you are unable to hold your focus, whether on your breath, a visualization, or some other object. But eventually, with practice, you are able to hold your object of meditation longer without distraction. When you have these three qualities of familiarity, not forgetting, and the ability to hold, then you can say that you are truly mindful.

The Three Methods of Resting in Meditation

Returning to the three stages of developing your meditation, the third stage is when you develop the three methods of resting in meditation: *resting, continual resting,* and *repeated resting.* If you prefer, you may remember these as: placement, continual placement, and repeated placement. There are nine ways of resting the mind described in Maitreya's *Mahayanasutralankara;* however, here we limit our discussion to the first three.

Resting the Mind

The first method, resting the mind, directly affects whatever comes next. In Tibetan, it is called *jokpa,* which means "to place" the mind on the object of meditation. Resting the mind means to take the mind and hold it to an object. For example, when you look at a beautiful statue of the Buddha, you may hold your attention on the Buddha's heart center; you put your mind there and leave it there. In a formal session, when you have begun to meditate, placement—or resting—is the first action performed. Therefore, it is the first of the three methods. When you begin the process of meditation, placing your mind is an important step in your learning. When you try to rest the mind by placing it on an object, you will experience the movement of your mind.

There are five different experiences (*movement, attainment, familiarity, stability,* and *consummation*) that you will encounter along your meditation journey. Here we will speak only about the main ones. The first experience is movement of the mind. The experience of discursiveness is important. When you try to place your mind or still it, you will notice its movement strongly—in a fresh, vivid way—as you are recognizing the movement of your mind for the first time. Your meditation is not creating any more thoughts or emotions than you had before, but now your awareness is noticing the movement.

Therefore, you are not able to hold your mind for very long on your object. You are starting to understand your mind more. That's very good!

The beginning of your meditation is just this: *dealing with your mind as it is*. As you become aware of your thoughts, you start to recognize who you are. When powerful thoughts arise, you will notice your mind becomes powerful. When you rest your mind, you will see where your mind actually is. Try to rest for as long as you are able, merely allowing your awareness to notice the stillness or movement of your mind.

The first method, resting—or placement—is just learning how the meditation practice works and developing the ability to meditate. That is how it begins. When your mind remains focused on the object and not many thoughts arise, then your mind becomes stabler and calmer. However, as a beginner, you won't be able to rest for a long time. If obstacles to your stability arise when you are meditating, the important point is the *moment of recognition*. If your mind is moving, your mind is thinking and engrossed in thought. Recognize this disturbance of your mind. You will see the movement easily because your mind is moving so much.

After you place your mind, you can have two different experiences that come from the movement of your mind. First, you can have the object of your focus in mind, but you notice that your mind is starting to wander away. This is when you need to practice the second method, continual resting. Second, you may become aware that you have completely lost your object of meditation. When this happens, practice the third method, repeated resting.

Continual Resting

The second method is continual resting or continual placement. In Tibetan, it is called *junjok*. This is practicing by prolonging the state of resting the mind by going further and deeper into your meditation. With your alert awareness, notice if your mindfulness is wavering. If so, bring it back to resting on your object of meditation before you completely lose the object. Hold your mind and maintain your mindfulness.

At this stage, you are still dealing with the movement of the mind. Through the ability to become familiar with both the stillness and the movement of your mind, you learn how to let go of your thoughts. Sometimes you will completely lose your object of focus and need to use your alert awareness to notice this. As you become more confident in your ability to rest in meditation, you will enjoy your practice and continually increase your stability.

Repeated Resting

When your mind moves and you completely lose your object, you need to practice the third method, repeated resting or repeated placement. The Tibetan word for this method is *lanjok*, meaning "to bring back," reconnect, and resettle the mind. When your mind loses its connection to its nature or object, you must bring it back and reconnect it.

The difference between the second and third method is that in the second method, you are not losing the object completely but you are very close to losing it, so you must continually rest. Otherwise you will lose it. In the third method, your mind has completely lost the object, so you need to reconnect your mind to the object again and again. You're learning repeated placement and how to repeatedly rest the mind. It's a small act, but it's one of the most courageous things you can do. When you recognize and try to release your thoughts, you will feel happy returning to the object again. Don't worry if you must do this thousands of times; this is why it is called practice.

In these methods of meditation, you are like a baby learning how to walk. Babies fall down repeatedly as they learn. Because they get up, take another step, fall down, and try again so many times, eventually they are able to walk continuously. It is the same when you are learning how to place your mind. At first your mind will stray almost every moment. But the more you bring it back, the more you will improve your ability to place the mind. Eventually you will be able to let your mind rest.

Each time you remember to place your mind on the object of your meditation, you are moving forward. The more you are able to strengthen your attention and focus, the stronger your mind, your experience, and the result become. When your mind wanders off, bring it back to the present again and again. In doing so, there is the possibility of your mind calming down and tuning in to its basic state of peace. The way to rest your mind in meditation is to let go of all thoughts. It doesn't matter whether the thoughts are positive or negative; let them go and just rest.

With this third method of repeated resting, you will have discursive thoughts, but you become more confident. Every time you recognize a thought, acknowledge it and let it go. This process makes your mind stronger. This is how you develop your shamatha meditation. There is no other way to do it.

Resting the mind, continuous resting, and repeated resting—these three methods work directly with your experiences to increase your ability to simply rest your mind in its natural state. These three methods help your mind to become stable. Based on that stability, you can develop other great experiences. As meditators, you must understand all these stages so that you can understand how to improve your meditation. Distraction is the main obstacle. Basically, when your mind is distracted, *you are not there.*

I collected these methods from different Buddhist texts and my experiences. When I practice shamatha, I use these methods as they are very helpful for my practice. Please keep them continuously in your mind as you meditate.

GUIDED PRACTICE:
SHAMATHA MEDITATION WITH OBJECT

There are various ways to practice shamatha meditation. Some methods use an object, and some do not. My experience is based on the instructions of Longchenpa, Mipham Rinpoche, and Adzom Drukpa Rinpoche. Here I have adapted their methods to be suitable for beginning meditators.

According to Adzom Drukpa Rinpoche's tradition—as found in earlier texts such as Longchenpa's fourteenth-century *Lama Yangtik Yishyin Norbu (The Quintessence of the Guru Wish-Fulfilling Jewel)*—a special method for producing extraordinary qualities is to practice shamatha meditation by resting the mind on a seed syllable. A seed syllable is the basis for visualizing a meditational deity. It is traditionally a Sanskrit or Tibetan letter in the alphabet.

If you don't know the traditional way to visualize seed syllables, you can use the equivalent Roman-script syllable (as described below)—or a pebble, blade of grass, piece of wood, or any object that is easy for you to visualize. What is most important is that whatever object you choose should appear clearly and steadily in your mind.

Meditation on the Syllable ཨ (A)

It is very beneficial to meditate on the white Tibetan seed syllable ཨ—or the Roman-script syllable A (prounounced AH)—as it symbolizes the birthlessness of all phenomena that is the embodiment of the nonconceptual wisdom minds of all the buddhas. My root teachers taught that by placing the mind on the white syllable A, one accomplishes samadhi and may attain the eight ordinary *siddhis*. These are the accomplishments that arise when a person successfully masters their mind via meditation training—for example, the siddhi of the pill that allows one to become invisible by holding the blessed pill in your hand.

In an isolated place, adjust your motivation by generating bodhichitta. With your body and mind peaceful and controlled, enter the meditative concentration of shamatha. Connect your breath with your awareness by visualizing a white Tibetan syllable ཨ or Roman-script syllable A at the tip of your nose. As you slowly exhale through your nose, visualize the white A going out with your breath and gradually expanding in size until it fills all of space. Fully rest your mind on the white syllable A. When you naturally inhale through your nose, visualize the white syllable A returning with your breath and gradually diminishing in size until it rests again on the tip of your nose. Meditate like this in frequent short sessions until your mind is still, thought does not interrupt your visualization, and you can focus single-pointedly on the white syllable A without distraction.

When you are meditating and notice your distracted mind, don't add more thoughts. Just notice your distraction; do not follow your thoughts. Let them go and rest your mind again on your object of meditation—the seed syllable. The fact that you are aware of your distraction means that your mindfulness is back. Rest in that awareness. Repeat this as often as necessary and know that over time, your mind will be able to rest naturally undistracted for longer periods due to your shamatha practice.

Meditation on the Syllable ཧཱུྃ (HŪṂ)

Another method for practicing shamatha is to focus your mind on the Tibetan syllable ཧཱུྃ or the Roman-script syllable HŪṂ (pronounced HUNG) and say the seed syllable aloud as you practice. As you did with the white syllable A, visualize the syllable HŪṂ going out and returning to the tip of your nose as you breathe in and out through your nose. As the seed syllable goes out, gently and softly recite HŪṂ with a long tone. Meditate like this repeatedly while visualizing your alert awareness as being of one nature with the syllable HŪṂ. When the syllable HŪṂ disappears and the sound of your HŪṂ vocalization stops, allow your mind to remain natural—and just rest. For as long as you can, don't think of anything.

If your body is too hot during the practice, you should meditate on the seed syllable and your breath as being as cold as ice; whereas if you are too cold, visualize it as being hot like fire.

When Mingyur Namkhe Dorje, the Fourth Dzogchen Rinpoche, was training in shamatha by practicing the syllable HŪṂ instructions, he saw all beings and worlds disappear into the seed syllable. When he arose from his meditation, the whole world and beings in his environment appeared in the aspect of the syllable HŪṂ. At that time, he was visualizing with such single-pointed concentration on the syllable HŪṂ that there was no duality between that syllable and the outer world— everything had merged with one taste into the syllable. This is due to the power of his meditation, not due to the power of the syllable.

When meditation with perfect concentration expands, one's samadhi can, without doubt, give rise to such appearances. Similarly, when Adzom Drukpa Rinpoche meditated on shamatha at an early age, he focused on a pigeon feather. After some time meditating like this, he could actually make a real feather go out from the tip of his nose and return to it.

Meditation on the Buddha

If you are a Buddhist, when you practice shamatha, you start by meditating with an object. The Buddha is the best object of focus. Begin by meditating on a radiant, golden-colored Buddha Shakyamuni in the space before you. Direct your alert awareness toward the Buddha's heart center. Don't allow anything to distract you; deeply relax and simply rest your mind on his heart center.

If thoughts arise, rest your mind again and practice continual resting. Don't follow your thoughts; just refocus your alert awareness on the Buddha's heart center. At the end of your meditation, with complete trust and devotion, imagine the Buddha melting into light and dissolving into you—your mind merging completely with the Buddha's mind.

Without following past thoughts or creating new thoughts, rest with your mind merged with the Buddha's mind. To accomplish meditative concentration, repeat this meditation frequently in short sessions. The benefit of this practice is stated in the *Samadhirajasutra*:

> Those who, while walking, sitting, standing, or sleeping, recollect the moonlike Buddha, will always be in Buddha's presence, and will attain the vast nirvana. And: his pure body is the color of gold, beautiful is the protector of the world. Whoever visualizes him like this practices the meditation of the bodhisattvas.

Meditation on the Tiklé

A third method of shamatha meditation is to visualize, at the point between your eyebrows, a pure white shining *tiklé*—a clear and brilliant sphere about the size of a pea—that appears yet lacks inherent existence. Rest your mind on it without distraction and allow your mind to settle naturally without thought. The visualized object—the shining tiklé—should be seen as possessing some weight and radiating light. Contemplating it as radiant prevents mental sinking and drowsiness, while contemplating it as having mass dispels mental agitation. If this doesn't alleviate sinking and excitement, sit facing a wall while you meditate to decrease mental distraction.

Mental sinking is caused by the mind being too withdrawn, gathered within, or depressed. A sinking mind is foggy and unclear. If it is sinking, your mind will lose its object of meditation and become unstable; you may even fall asleep. To remedy this, elevate your mind by recalling things that give you joy and resume your shamatha practice. Mental agitation occurs when your mind is distracted by external objects or too many thoughts. The remedy for mental agitation is to be alert and to draw your mind within. Make your adjustments and settle your mind again on your object of meditation. I will explain more about these two obstacles shortly.

Meditation on the Three Channels

Another very profound method to accomplish meditative concentration is to take the three subtle channels, the *nadi*, as your meditation object. The three channels are the central channel (*uma*), which runs parallel to the spine; and the right channel (*roma*) and the left channel (*kyangma*), which run on either side of the central channel.

Generally the colors and directions of these channels depend on gender and meditation. For this meditation, you visualize your body as a clear-light body with the right channel as white, the left channel as red, and the central channel as blue in color. Visualize the upper ends of the right and left channels coming from the openings of your right and left nostrils and running down through your body, with their lower ends merging into the central channel below your navel. The central channel is slightly wider than the right and left channels. In this case, visualize the central channel as clear, straight, and upright in the middle of your body. Visualize its lower tip ending at your navel and its upper tip going up to the level of your heart. Visualize at your heart center a white seed syllable A or a white, radiant sphere, a tiklé.

Inhaling very slowly and gently through your nostrils, visualize your breath flowing down through the right and left channels and entering the central channel below your navel; your breath merges where the right and left channels join the central channel. Your breath then travels up through the central channel to your heart center. When it arrives at your heart center, the breath merges with the white seed syllable A (or the tiklé), causing it to radiate more brightly. Focus your alert awareness on your breath and the seed syllable merged as one, settle in meditative equipoise, and let go of your thoughts. When your thoughts move, repeat the visualization frequently in short sessions.

Traditional Tibetan medical treatises explain how the countless root and branch subtle channels arise in dependence upon the potential and function of these three channels. The tantric texts explain that the body-mind develops and exists in its coarse form based on the indivisible subtle nature of the channels.

We cannot see the three channels in our body with our physical eyes because they do not exist in coarse form. Yet they are the pathways for the relative red and white essences (the tiklé) and the subtle wind energies (the *lung*) that are the indispensable first parts to form as a human body develops. When an embryo is conceived in the womb, three things must be established simultaneously— the fathers's sperm (the white essence), the mother's blood (the red essence), and the indivisible subtle energy of the mind. The central channel is the basis for the generation and ripening of the wind energies; these, in turn, are the principal ripeners of the sperm and the blood. To the right of the blue central channel (*uma*) is the white channel (*kyangma*) that is the basis for the increase of the white essence—the water element. To the left of the blue central channel is the red channel (*roma*) that is the basis for the ripening of the red essence—the fire element.

Meditation on the Breath in Three Stages

Another effective method of shamatha meditation is to practice breathing in three stages, focusing on the inbreath, the out-breath, and the gap or pause between these two. Relatively, you can release all physical and mental suffering and achieve peace of mind by meditating with your breath. Ultimately, you can realize wisdom through these methods.

When you focus on your breath, it happens only in the present moment. If you practice mindfulness and appreciate training with your breath, you will have an incredible number of opportunities to balance your body and mind every day.

To do this meditation, relax your body and mind. Breathe in very gently and then pause your breath below the area of your navel. Relax every part of your body and mind on your breath held gently below the navel. When you must exhale, naturally let your breath go. When you are gently holding your breath below your navel, let your breath dissolve into your mind and look deeply into your own nature. Try looking at the mind that is aware and rest there. Do not follow thoughts about the past or future. Just remain in the present moment.

Keep your mind placed on your breath, remaining aware of the presence of your breath. When your mind is distracted, gently bring it back to your breath and leave it there. Leave your body relaxed. As you pay attention to your breathing, you will be aware of sounds and thoughts. Do not grasp or reject them; just leave them alone.

With all your strength, focus your mind on your breath resting in the space of your body below your navel. Repeat this process again and again. Breathe in, gently hold your air below your navel, and gently breathe out. Rest your alert awareness on each stage of your breath. As you do this meditation, slowly allow yourself to enter more deeply into quiet and calm. Just let yourself be in alert awareness.

Be aware of the gap between your inbreath and outbreath. Between these two, you will experience inner calm. Relax in that space. When you breathe in and out, simply concentrate on your breath. When you pause your breath, relax into your experience, recognizing the natural peacefulness in between your inbreath and outbreath.

As a beginning meditator, you will experience this peaceful-ness. If you are more advanced, you will experience the ground consciousness—that is, the *alaya*. If you are the highest level of practitioner, you will experience the nature of mind—ultimate bodhichitta. This meditation is profoundly simple and helpful for all levels of meditators.

If you practice for a long time, your body and mind may become tired, and you will not feel like meditating. Go to a pleasant, isolated place—to the mountains or a beach, for example—to relax your body and mind. This will help your meditation.

GUIDED PRACTICE:
SHAMATHA MEDITATION WITHOUT OBJECT

Mipham Rinpoche states that if the previously explained meditation methods do not stop the proliferation of thought, we should practice objectless shamatha meditation. There are different methods of shamatha meditation without objects or signs, the most profound of which is called *mind looking at mind*. This means we should not follow our thoughts; instead, we should recognize them as soon as they arise by abiding inseparably with mindfulness and alertness. When mind looks at mind, all the thoughts of the past or future stop. This method to develop shamatha is an essential instruction for all other types of meditation that involve resting one's mind.

To meditate in this way, relax your body and mind. With a motivation inseparable from bodhichitta, neither follow your thoughts nor allow your mind to become attached to any object. Let your mind settle naturally just as it is. Don't pursue or hold on to recurring thoughts about the past; don't welcome thoughts about the future. On the basis of the present moment, abide free of all thought, remaining in a nonconceptual state as long as you can.

If you become distracted by positive, negative, or neutral thoughts, immediately apply mindfulness and alertness. Then visualize your guru, who embodies all sources of refuge, in the space before you. With deep faith and devotion, make a heartfelt aspiration prayer and request your guru to bless you to develop special realization of the profound path in that very moment! Then return to the state of your meditative concentration as before.

The Achievement of Shamatha

As Kamalashila says,

> You should understand that calm abiding is actualized when
> you enjoy physical and mental pliancy through prolonged
> familiarity with the meditation, and the mind gains the
> power to engage the object as it chooses.

If your body and mind become so well trained that your mind can remain focused on an object as long as you wish, then shamatha meditation has been attained. Great masters, who have developed their shamatha, can stop all discursive thought and remain in a nonconceptual state for as long as they wish—even months or years—with an unmoving body and mind. It is said that Milarepa meditated day and night for six months in the presence of his guru Marpa to develop shamatha meditation.

When the mind can remain still and focused like a calm ocean, that is the culmination of meditative concentration. At that point, without effort, your mind naturally enters samadhi and you can remain focused on your object as long as you wish. This is called *the single-pointed mind of the desire realm.* When this mind develops, then delusions, such as attachment and aversion, are weakened and fewer thoughts arise.

Experiences of bliss, clarity, and nonthought begin from this point. For example, while meditating you might experience a great sensation of bliss—your mind is happy and peaceful. Your body is relaxed—you feel like you could stay like that for many days without moving. You feel a very subtle pleasant sensation. This pleasure and comfort are what we call the experience of bliss.

At the same time, you might also experience a great clarity that arises in your meditation. You might feel like you know what will happen in the future and sometimes your body will feel very light. Sometimes you might feel like you can fly or that you do not have a body. This is the experience of clarity. This clarity brings great wisdom and the ability to know what the future holds.

You may feel like you have no thoughts and abide easily in a state of equanimity without distraction. If you have thoughts, they suddenly dissolve—and you can remain continuously in meditation for a long time. As your ability to meditate develops, your mind becomes more and more settled. You become confident in your meditation at this point. These are the three kinds of experiences that can arise when you meditate with concentration.

Although many different experiences arise from this type of meditative concentration, it is important not to be attached to them. The great master Khenchen Jigme Phuntsok taught these three experiences in detail when he gave the Dzogchen teaching on Patrul Rinpoche's commentary on *Striking the Vital Point in Three Statements*, and he advised that even if we have special experiences, we must not become filled with pride or arrogance. Therefore, it is important to receive genuine teachings from an experienced teacher who can point out the possible pitfalls of these experiences.

When you meditate like this, your mind becomes flexible and workable, such that you can focus it on an object at will; and your body feels extremely light and pervaded by bliss. When your body and mind are completely workable, without any disturbance, you have developed the genuine meditative concentration of shamatha. At that point, you can successfully do any type of meditation—for example, on the generation and completion stages of the Vajrayana or Dzogchen meditation. Thus, shamatha meditation is the foundation for all other meditation, and it is important to practice it first.

Obstacles to Meditation and Their Remedies

There are a lot of obstacles when you meditate, but most of them are a type of dullness or restless agitation. If you take care of these two general obstacles immediately when they arise, you will be cutting the roots of most common obstacles to accomplishing your practice.

When you first begin to practice, you should meditate frequently for short periods of time. As a beginning practitioner, if you try to practice for a long time, two obstacles will arise: dullness (drowsiness) and agitation (distraction). Subtle and gross forms of these states will arise as obstacles, hindering the power of your practice.

If you meditate, your mind may sink into unclear dullness; you may feel like you want to sleep. The sooner you catch your drowsiness, the easier it is to counteract. There are many effective antidotes developed by great meditators to remedy dullness. One is to engage more fully with your breath by taking a few deep breaths. Another is to open your alert awareness and allow external sounds and sensations in. A third antidote is to straighten your spine by adjusting your sitting position. In addition, you may wish to meditate on your good fortune by remembering that you have a precious human life with the freedom to practice.

If you are meditating with your eyes closed, try opening your eyes fully and letting light in, then meditate for a while with your eyes open. Rub and squeeze your hands several times. Clench your whole body and release it. Stand up, stretch, and move your body vigorously for a while. Try splashing water on your face and slapping your forehead. These remedies will help you to wake up from dullness or drowsiness so that you can return to meditating with your full energy and power.

If you meditate and your mind is restless and distracted, you will not be able to focus on the object. This is another obstacle to meditation. One antidote to agitation and distraction is to engage more fully with your object. Alternatively, focus your alert awareness on sensations at your abdomen or your heart center. An especially powerful way to get ahold of your mind is to reflect that death is certain but the time of death is uncertain. This rouses you to focus and practice before it is too late. Thinking about the impermanence of life and uncertainty of the time of death will encourage you to not delay your practice; remembering this will help to focus and keep your mind calm. Right now, your mind is restless and roaming all over the place, so you should think about something that brings your mind back to the essence of what is meaningful in your life. The awareness you gain when contemplating impermanence can be useful to your meditation practice when your mind is agitated or distracted.

When you meditate, as with any important activity, you need a certain amount of motivation to complete what you start. If you experience benefit and joy in what you are doing, then you will want to continue until you attain your goal. However, as mentioned before, do not expect immediate results. No matter how long you meditate, even for five minutes, try to meditate with a fresh, vivid, alert mind; try to maintain single-pointed concentration without being distracted by thoughts. Otherwise, if you are just sitting on your cushion and thinking, then your mind will wander all over; it will not rest in alert awareness. Of course, it happens naturally when you meditate that thoughts arise suddenly. Rather than following the thoughts, immediately bring your mind back through mindfulness. Factors that hinder the development of samadhi are laziness, engaging in too many activities, being distracted by many thoughts of the past or future, and having a foggy mind in which appearances and awareness lack clarity. These are obstructions to samadhi, so it is important to use appropriate antidotes when they occur. Remember the antidotes to dullness and agitation mentioned here.

Finally, to accomplish concentration in meditation, you need devotion, joyful effort, mindfulness, and alert awareness. Without these, concentration is impossible. At the root of all meditation is proper motivation: remember your kind heart of bodhichitta and rouse yourself again and again to do your best to benefit all living beings, including yourself. To summarize:

Shamatha is the method to correctly stop appearances
of our completely out-of-control mind.
Although not the direct cause of ultimate liberation,
when thoughts are pacified through shamatha, our mind is
    under control.

10

Introduction to Vipashyana

The perfect meditative concentration of shamatha alone does not eliminate delusion from the root or prevent its recurrence. The mind is only temporarily isolated from thought. When difficult circumstances are encountered, thoughts will arise again. Like muddy water that has settled, it appears temporarily clean and pure, but because it is not separated from the silt, as soon as it is stirred up, it becomes muddy again. Thus accomplishment of shamatha alone cannot cause all attachment and delusions to be abandoned from the root—it can only suppress them. As Kamalashila says,

> By doing only shamatha meditation, yogins do not abandon the obscurations; it only suppresses them for a while. Without the arising of the appearance of wisdom, the delusions remain dormant and it is impossible to destroy them—so they will not be destroyed.

Therefore, to abandon delusions from the root, it is necessary to practice shamatha inseparable from vipashyana. Vipashyana means *to look directly and clearly with insight.* When our mind is unmoving, we may have the meditative concentration of nonconceptual shamatha, but if we do not have the insightful wisdom realizing emptiness, then no matter how long we meditate, we cannot realize how phenomena exist.

As is said in Kamalashila's *Stages of Meditation* and other texts, without having the view that understands emptiness and a meditative concentration that remains effortlessly focused upon it, discursive thoughts will disturb our subtle wind energies (*lung*) and it will be impossible to clearly see the ultimate nature, the actual mode of existence of the phenomena that appear to our mind.

The Sanskrit word *vi* means "special" or "particular"; *pashyana* means "to see" or "to look." Therefore, vipashyana means to look at things in a very direct and clear way. The sutras also say that vipashyana has the clarity of understanding in which everything is seen clearly and distinctly. So, the actual nature of things is seen *as it is*—this is what is meant by vipashyana. It is necessary to have the viewpoint of the absence of self. Without this viewpoint, we cannot develop genuine vipashyana meditation. Therefore, we must develop this understanding of the absence of self. As Chandrakirti says,

> If self exists, other is known. Then there arises clinging to my
> side and aversion to others. It is in connection with this that
> all faults arise.

The desire for our own happiness and freedom from suffering—attachment to our side and aversion to another's point of view—is the root of all faults and problems. Our problems exist as long we are strongly attached to our selfish interests. We believe that we inherently exist and, through the force of grasping at an inherently existent self, we cling to objects that we believe will make us happy. The desire for wealth, praise, and other worldly pleasures arises from the root of self-grasping. If we have these in our life, we believe we are happy. If we do not, we suffer.

When delusions develop, they develop in relationship to an object. Attachment develops toward pleasant objects and aversion toward unpleasant objects—with ignorance as the basis of both. This is what we call *self-grasping ignorance.* The stronger our self-grasping, the more likely we are to perform strongly negative actions to obtain our goals. When we understand the essential points of dependent origination, hold the view of emptiness, and recognize natural awareness, our convictions in these teachings and our realization protect us from suffering. We will cherish others' well-being and act toward them with nothing but kindness and love.

Emptiness and dependent arising are inseparable. If we don't realize this inseparability, we don't have the recognition of the nature of emptiness. When we say that the mind is empty, it doesn't mean that our mind doesn't exist or it is like empty space with nothing in it. The mind as emptiness has the ability to understand everything; it is cognizant and knowing. It's like a crystal that is clear yet perfectly reflects all appearances without bias. Our mind is like that crystal—pure and clear—yet all appearances can arise in it. This knowing quality of the mind is what we call *self-arising wisdom.*

Our nature is pure and good. As I mentioned earlier, as ordinary beings who have not recognized fully our buddha nature, we are like a window with dirt on it; the dirt is temporarily obscuring our clear view. However, the dirt is neither inherent to the window nor is it its nature. As we clean the window, we get a clear view of what's outside the window. Our mind is just like that. It's not intrinsically stained. As we practice, we will reveal our basic goodness—our natural purity that we refer to as buddha nature. Your nature is pure and radiant. Look into your own mind to see if this is true based on your experience.

If you understand reality, everything arises spontaneously. Then you simply rest and develop your capacity to abide in your natural awareness (*rigpa*) continuously. You will clearly be aware of this openness that we call self-arising awareness. There is no buddha other than this. You can recognize this perfect buddha in your mind now. As Dudjom Rinpoche says in *Spontaneous Song of the Genuine Nature: A Prayer Calling the Guru from Afar*,

> Since this present awareness is the actual buddha,
> I find the guru of openness and contentment within my heart.
> When I realize that this genuine mind is the very nature of
>   the guru,
> there is no need for attached and grasping prayers or artificial
>   complaints.
> By relaxing in uncontrived awareness, the free and open
>   natural state,
> I obtain the blessing of the aimless self-liberation of whatever
>   arises.

The Two Selflessnesses

Chandrakirti says that from the ordinary point of view, there is nothing we need to debate about, as everything works just as it is. However, if we want to understand the ultimate level, then we must change our view and investigate deeply. What we call *self* is a combination of ever-changing physical and mental forces or energies, which are divided into five groups or aggregates. What does this mean? It means the aggregates are like building materials—stone, wood, and other things that are necessary to build a structure.

Similarly, the aggregates determine the nature of what we call *me* or *I*. Because aggregates have come together due to karmic forces, our appearance arises. Our collection of aggregates form the condition that has made our appearance possible. Due to the nature of this appearance, a sense of self or me has arisen. This idea of I gives rise to self-interest—the sense of me here and everything and everyone else out there. This is the deception of the dualistic mind.

Self-grasping ignorance has two types: grasping at the *self of persons* and grasping at the *self of phenomena*. Self-grasping ignorance arises in relation to the combination of the five ever-changing physical and mental energies—the aggregates—that make up our world. If we observe any of the aggregates of our continuum and label them as a self, an I—a permanent, partless, independent, self-sufficient entity—this is grasping at the self of persons. If we analyze our projection of an I onto the five psychophysical aggregates of form, feeling, perception, formations, and consciousness, we will recognize that I is merely a label and not valid. Upon examination, we will find that our I, or self, is merely designated in relationship to the collection of the aggregates.

This superimposition is what is perceived as truly existent, but in fact it is not. The mind that superimposes an I merely grasps at its conceived object, a self—like mistaking a striped rope for a snake in dim light. The multicolored rope is similar to our five aggregates—the dim darkness is the deceptive confusion of our ignorance, and seeing the snake is like grasping at a self or I. When we recognize the rope, the mind apprehending the snake stops. Likewise, if we realize that the self, or I, exists neither inside, nor outside, nor in between, this recognition stops our ignorant self-grasping.

If a self, or I, existed inherently, it would be either the same as or different from the aggregates. Other than this, there is no way that a self, or I, could exist. If the self, or I, was the same as the aggregates, then it would be multiple and impermanent like the aggregates. Yet self and the aggregates are not different entities because they are mutually dependent—one cannot exist without the other. When we search for a distinct, independent, permanent self inside or outside the five aggregates, we cannot find it, as it does not exist.

If someone claims that consciousness, one of the five aggregates, is the self, then you must remind them that past consciousness has ceased and future awareness has not arisen. The current moment of awareness arises and ceases in an instant. Because a self is defined as permanent, consciousness cannot be a self.

A permanent self cannot be found in the awareness of past, present, or future. Like a chariot that is designated merely in dependence upon its parts—the axles, wheels, and so on—the chariot does not inherently exist in any of its parts or in the collection of them. In the same manner, the mistaken mind of self-grasping merely imputes a self onto the collection of the aggregates; self does not exist inherently by way of its own entity but arises in dependence upon ignorance. When we realize the absence of the true existence of the aggregates, we realize the selflessness of the person. This stops the grasping at a personal identity, an I. If we have no self-grasping, we do not create negativity, as all our actions are motivated by kindness and compassion. The amount of negativity in our lives is directly related to the amount of self-grasping ignorance that we possess.

To realize the selflessness of phenomena, we need to realize the emptiness of all outer and inner phenomena, from their grossest to their subtlest levels. Phenomena merely appear as discrete, independent entities; but if we analyze them, we cannot find any inherent existence in them. They do not exist as singular phenomena or as multiple phenomena; nor do they exist as one or as many. For example, gross phenomena can only be posited relative to subtle phenomena. Similarly, one depends on many, and vice versa. Ultimately there is no dividing line between them. When causes and conditions momentarily come together, things appear—like reflections in a mirror or appearances in a dream. They do not inherently exist yet they appear unfailingly due to dependent origination.

Many different assertions are made by non-Buddhists to justify the concept of the independent self or soul. Some believe that there is a self that goes from this life to future lives, experiencing the results of good and bad karma. But if we examine phenomena clearly, including our notions about ourselves, we can observe that phenomena do not inherently exist because they arise based on interdependence alone. There is no contradiction between phenomena *appearing conventionally* and their *being empty of inherent existence*. Cause and effect, interdependence, and emptiness are complementary. The *Heart Sutra* says,

Form is emptiness; emptiness is form. Form is not other than emptiness, emptiness is not other than form.

These four statements indicate that the ultimate nature of form—earth, water, fire, and wind—is emptiness appearing as *nondual reality*. When we investigate, we see that emptiness and dependent arising are interchangeable. This view of appearance-emptiness is called *the great view of the Middle Way school*, as it is free from fabrication. As phenomena appear relatively, the view is free from the extreme of nihilism. As phenomenal appearances are empty of inherent existence, the view is free from the extreme of permanence. As the Buddha Shakyamuni states in the *Samadhirajasutra*,

Existence and nonexistence are extremes,
purity and impurity are extremes as well,
thus, having relinquished both extremes,
the wise do not dwell even in the middle.

When we analyze with logic, we recognize that although phenomena appear, they do not inherently exist; they are baseless and rootless. To realize the ultimate view of Dzogchen, the great equality of dharmata, we must, according to the oral instructions of our guru, deepen our understanding of the union of appearance and emptiness until we experience the clear-light mind in which all mental fabrications are completely stilled.

Destroying Wrong Views

We have many illusory, mistaken views. For example, we think that something is a single entity, when it isn't. When we think of our body, we think of it as a single whole. However, if we analyze it, we find that our body is made of many parts. For example, the traditional Buddhist analogy is to look at all the parts of a chariot, but for us, let's think about our car. Your car is made of many parts, such as wheels, the steering wheel, and so forth. If any part is not functioning, your vehicle doesn't work. Each part is dependent on the others to be labeled a car that is drivable. This is what meditators do to destroy the wrong view of the belief in a permanent single whole.

To compare this to our own form, if we continue to investigate our body—not only investigate but meditate on the results of our investigation—we will destroy our concept of body. Doing this helps us destroy attachment to our body. If we don't investigate, we will continue to misperceive reality, viewing compounded phenomena as a singular body or entity. Believing in this type of illusion, we cannot destroy self-grasping. We will relate to the world through our mistaken concepts rather than according to how it is actually arising.

Therefore, we must investigate our body and destroy our idea of self-existence. If we do this, we will see that the true nature of our body is emptiness—it's dependently arising moment by moment in relationship with everything. We don't have this view because we are ignorant, relying as we do on superficial, mistaken concepts of what is. Believing in single uncompounded entities, such as *myself* or *my body*, we mistakenly perceive impermanent things to be permanent.

Do you remember what you did yesterday? You might respond by saying, *I did this and that yesterday*, believing that yesterday's you and today's you are the same person. Your ego holds a permanent concept of your ordinary self all the time—you tell yourself marvelous stories such as: *This year, last year, the year before, I did this and I did that.* From the

Buddhist point of view, your ego's interpretation is unreasonable; it is pure fiction. It is a nice story, but it has nothing whatsoever to do with reality. Your ego is simply holding on to the idea of self-existence. Dharmakshita, one of Atisha's gurus, states in his *Wheel of Sharp Weapons*,

All things are like images found in a mirror,
and yet we imagine they are real, very real;
all things are like mist or like clouds on a mountain,
and yet we imagine they are stable and firm.
Our foe, our insistence on ego identities
truly our own, which we wish were secure,
and our butcher: the selfish concern for ourselves—
like all things these appear to be truly existent,
though they never have been truly existent at all.

Although they appear to be concrete and real,
they have never been real, anytime, anywhere.
They are not things we should burden with ultimate value,
nor should we deny them their relative truth.

Therefore, we mistakenly think something is permanent when it is not—that it is unchanging and, in fact, unchangeable. However, that is not how things are; everything is changing all the time. But due to our mistaken views, no matter how much change there is, we still believe that we and our environment are permanent. If we realize that these wrong views and ordinary ideas are mistaken, then the understanding of our precious human life, the impermanence of life, and cause and effect (karma) will develop easily. This is very important as it can destroy our destructive thoughts and the mistakes that are the root and source of our problems.

When we realize the emptiness of self and the emptiness of phenomena, the power of the dualistic mind shatters. Like a thief in an empty house, we find nothing to steal—there is no illusion of a subject or an object to grasp. Our delusion, attachment, aversion, and karma end when our fundamental ignorance is shattered. We no longer lose our freedom, undergo great suffering, or wander in endless cycles of suffering in samsara because the causes of those states are cut. When the roots of deluded grasping are severed, we experience liberation from mistaken views. This is good news.

If we are ready to release self-grasping, then emptiness is there already. Sometimes we are quite uncertain what emptiness actually is. It is connected with the attainment of enlightenment that transcends or goes beyond dualistic perceptions. The ultimate reality is not separate from us; we live it all the time. Therefore, it is not somewhere beyond the sky. It is like the wave and water. A wave can be high or low, but the wave is always made of water. When we realize the ultimate nature of reality correctly, then we are free from everything—all our fabricated notions about enlightenment dissolve like Dharmarakshita's mist or clouds on a mountain.

When we look deeply into our mind, we have basic goodness—our buddha nature. Buddha nature is the ability to understand and touch our real nature. When we look at the sky and see thick clouds, we can't see the sun, but we can infer that the sun is there. When the clouds dissolve, we can see the sun. Just like that, it is possible to trust that we will be able to awaken to the nature of our mind when our dualistic mind has dissolved into our enlightened essence—our buddha nature.

GUIDED PRACTICE:
ANALYTICAL MEDITATION ON SELFLESSNESS

Analytical meditation on selflessness focuses on the deep interconnection between mind and body, which is to see things as they truly are. It is the oldest Buddhist meditation practice.

Visualize in the space before you all the buddhas, bodhisattvas, and the spiritual beings who most inspire you. Request them to bless you with their compassion and wisdom by reciting: "In order to obtain the state of enlightenment for the benefit of all living beings, I shall meditate on selflessness. Bless me and all living beings to realize the ultimate selflessness of phenomena."

Then visualize before you the object to which you are most attached, such as your own body. Meditate on this question: *What are the characteristics of this body that I conceive of and cling to without interruption? Searching this form carefully inside and outside, I resolve to see if I can find anything that exists independently, on its own.*

Starting with the top of your head, begin the process of analytical meditation by asking yourself, *Is my hair my head? Is my scalp my head? Is my skull my head? Is my brain my head?* Similarly, continue to check your eyes, ears, nose, lips, tongue, and so on to see if they are your head. Notice that if each body part were your head, you would have many heads! However, you do not consider this to be the case, do you? If none of these parts are your head, where will you find your true head?

Realize that you have superimposed a concept of head onto a collection of parts. You could continue to break down these gross parts into subtler parts, such as molecules or atoms, if you wished. Similarly, they would be exhausted under analysis. By examining and meditating on all phenomena repeatedly in this way, you develop the view of selflessness.

Just as you examined and searched for the true location of your head, you should continue your analytical meditation with every part of your body. If you had a pile of grain mixed together, you could examine each part to see if it was wheat, barley, or rye. Similarly, examine the elements of your body to see which part contains your true self. Follow the advice of Mipham Rinpoche:

When meditating this way, if other thoughts arise, don't fall prey to them. Place your mind back upon its previous object. Search sometimes for your own body and aggregates or, at other times, depending upon what is easier, search for another's body and aggregates.

Meditate in this way repeatedly. When you are certain that your form aggregate does not inherently exist, examine whether the other four aggregates—sensations, perceptions, formations, and consciousness—exist. After you have completed your investigation of your own five aggregates, examine other phenomena. If after much meditation you become exhausted, let your mind settle naturally and let go of any thought. When you feel refreshed or when your thoughts begin to arise again, return to your analytical meditation as before—alternate between short periods of resting meditation and short periods of analytical meditation.

If you continue this process to fruition, your self-grasping ignorance will diminish, your experience of well-being and contentment will increase naturally, and you will realize self-lessness and emptiness. Concurrently, compassion for those who don't recognize the nature of reality will become boundless—a great love for living beings, without discrimination, will arise in you.

GUIDED PRACTICE:
RESTING VIPASHYANA MEDITATION

With resting vipashyana meditation, the mind is not focused on anything—it rests in a completely stable, relaxed, and unwavering state. When thoughts arise, look at the nature of the thoughts and recognize that these thoughts are nothing other than a manifestation of the nature of mind. Recognize the nature of your thoughts and let them naturally dissolve into the nature of your mind. Then relax in that space as much as you can. Like the waves in the ocean, let your thoughts dissolve naturally.

If you think about a wave, it is just the movement of the ocean—nothing exists other than that. Similarly, your thoughts are just the movement of the nature of your mind—nothing exists other than that. When they arise, recognize that they are inseparable from awareness and emptiness. Meditate on this.

During meditation, different feelings and thoughts will arise. The great masters instruct us to rest in our nature—do not try to stop your thoughts or follow them. It does not matter what kind of thoughts arise or how many times your mind wanders away. Whatever you see, whatever you hear, whatever arises—simply leave it as it is. Rest your mind in its nature and continue to relax your mind without losing your self-awareness. Keep that self-awareness and relaxation in your mind constantly. The Dzogchen lineage masters advise meditators to leave four things naturally as they are:

View, like a mountain, leave it as it is.
Meditation, like an ocean, leave it as it is.
Action, appearances, leave them as they are.
Fruition, rigpa, leave it as it is.

Similarly, the great yogin Tilopa says to stop all physical activity and remain naturally at ease. Do not think about anything; look at experience beyond thought. Vipashyana meditation arises naturally once we recognize our true nature. It is not something that we can do; it is something that must happen spontaneously when we rest our mind naturally with self-awareness. That is what we mean by resting vipashyana meditation.

The Difference between Shamatha and Vipashyana

We develop shamatha by resting our mind on an external object such as a statue of the Buddha or on an internal object such as our breath. We can also develop it without an object when we meditate using our mind to look directly at our mind and so on. This practice makes the mind still and calm. Having developed shamatha in this way, we practice vipashyana next by analyzing and examining the mind to develop an understanding of the inseparability of awareness and emptiness.

The difference between shamatha and vipashyana is that while shamatha is resting without thought, vipashyana is recognizing the clarity of the mind. The meditative concentration of shamatha arises when you can remain single-pointedly focused on an observed object; vipashyana is the wisdom realizing selflessness—a transcendent wisdom free of perceiving any observed object as having inherent existence. That is what we call the union of shamatha and vipashyana meditation.

The great teacher Milarepa gave us three examples of how to practice the union of shamatha and vipashyana. When you look at the sky, there is no center and no edge that you can point to; however, clouds may appear in the sky. If you look at a mountain, it is completely stable and unmoving; however, plants and trees may grow on the mountain. If you look at the ocean, it is completely calm; however, waves may still appear. In the same way, your mind is calm and clear; however, thoughts may appear. If you are able to meditate on the mind, your thoughts will appear, but they are just movements of the mind.

They are just manifestations of the energy of the mind. If you understand the nature of thoughts, they will naturally disappear.

In this way, we can understand the union of shamatha and vipashyana. Resting without thought is shamatha meditation; knowing that these thoughts are nothing other than manifestations of the mind is vipashyana meditation. The key point in vipashyana meditation is awareness. It is simply a state of mind that is not distracted from the present moment. When we bring the mind to rest in its own state, in its own nature, without distraction, then we are in a state of awareness of the present moment.

Mipham Rinpoche says that you do not need to make the mind clear or improve the nature of your mind. The nature of your mind is always perfect. For example, a very sharp sword that is put away in its sheath cannot cut anything, but when you take the sword out, it already has the ability to cut. This ability is not taken away by putting it in its sheath. Similarly, your mind is covered with afflictions and obscurations, so you cannot recognize the nature of mind. However, as soon as you remove the obscurations, the nature of mind is already radiant and perfect. It arises and manifests within the space of your awareness in its natural state.

The details of these practices should be received from your root teacher. When you receive these instructions directly from your guru, it is a much more personal and powerful experience. The moment of transmission—of pointing out the nature of mind—becomes a genuine powerful meeting of minds. The instructions are far more effective than when you receive a general introduction to vipashyana meditation from a book. When you receive pointing-out instructions from your root teacher, you will be introduced directly and nakedly to the reality of your mind's nature. When you have fully recognized the nature of your mind, from then on you will no longer undergo great suffering or have to wander in endless cycles of suffering in samsara. To summarize:

If we analyze it, whatever appears is mind's manifestation.
Mind free of extremes is the great Middle Way.
Conceiving inexpressible mind to be a self
has caused us to wander until now in samsara.

11

The Guru-Disciple Relationship and How to Receive Empowerments

Empowerment is the first door to entering the practice of tantra. Therefore, the path of Vajrayana must be attained in dependence upon empowerment, as advised by great teachers, such as Khenchen Tsultrim Lodrö. A person who has not received empowerment is not permitted to listen to or undertake the actual tantric practices. If one intends to practice Vajrayana, the first step must be to receive an empowerment. Therefore, it is important to explain a little bit about the meaning of empowerment, when you should or should not take it, and what are the causes and conditions needed by both the teacher and disciple to give and receive a perfect empowerment.

Presently there are two problems with empowerments: First, practitioners do not know what qualifications the person conferring the empowerment and the person receiving the empowerment should possess, nor what is expected of them prior to and during empowerment.

For example, if the vajra master conferring the empowerment is not qualified, the empowerment will not be complete; it may even cause the person at the other end not to receive it. Second, practitioners do not know what is expected of them after the empowerment. Here I would like to remind everyone that, after the empowerment, we must study the fourteen root tantric precepts, or the precepts that correspond with the empowerment, and keep our vows.

The Tibetan word for a tantric empowerment (*wang*)—Sanskrit (*abhisheka*)—means both "to destroy" and "to pour." During the profound ritual of a Vajrayana empowerment, all obscurations of body, speech, and mind are destroyed when wisdom is poured into the mind of the disciple. The Vajrayana path requires empowerment from a vajra master to authorize a practitioner to receive the profound instructions that have the power to ripen and liberate one's mindstream within one lifetime.

The great master Yukhok Chatral Chöying Rangdrol describes empowerment as authorizing a prince to take control of the kingdom; through a Vajrayana empowerment, the body is ripened into the yidam deity, a chosen tutelary meditational deity; the speech is ripened into mantra; and the thoughts within the mind are ripened into transcendent wisdom. Because of empowerment's capacity to swiftly transform reality, it is important to analyze the vajra master before you receive empowerment from them to ensure that you have genuine faith in the lineage teachings that you will receive and that you will be able to uphold the commitments of this path.

Empowerments have the potential for great benefit and great danger. Like a snake that enters a bamboo pole has nowhere to go but straight up or down, similarly a student who enters the Secret Mantrayana—the vehicle of Tibetan Buddhism that uses the union of skillful means and wisdom to protect the mind from ordinary, dualistic perception—without a strong foundation may go down a path that is not suitable for them. Thus, due to its power, this vehicle is traditionally kept secret. It is not because tantra has some fault that must be hidden. It is kept secret from disciples of lesser capacity to protect them from practices for which they are not prepared. If they encounter it prematurely, they may, unfortunately, turn from this profound path toward a lesser one due to confusion.

For special trainees of the sharpest faculties, however, Mantrayana is a much swifter path; it is rich in skillful means and yields the fruit of buddhahood without hardship. Just as precious things, such as gold and silver, are held in the hands of the rich, not the poor, only someone who is very blessed and fortunate can engage in the extremely precious and profound teachings of the Secret Mantrayana. Therefore, if a trainee is not wise enough to practice at their own level, it can be dangerous.

If an arrogant teacher gives empowerments just for the sake of fame and pretends to introduce disciples to Dzogchen, mahamudra, or other profound views without having maintained their own commitments, it is best for them to desist. It is also best for disciples not to receive empowerment if they don't possess renunciation and bodhichitta, have no meditation experience, or, even worse, have no faith or belief in the profound meaning of tantra. The type of empowerment where the disciple has not taken refuge vows, for example, holds no power.

The most important points and requirements of a disciple, Khenchen Tsultrim Lodrö says, are summarized in these five:

First, renunciation; second, bodhichitta; third, faith; fourth, comprehension of the teachings in the initiation and ability to visualize the deity and mandala during the initiation; and fifth, ability to uphold the tantric precepts after the empowerment.

If any of these points is missing, one cannot receive empowerment at all. The great master Drukpa Kunleg jokes,

The lama conferring empowerment explains the Dharma: "There is nothing in my mind! *Samaya!*" Disciples, with closed eyes and folded palms, repeat, "There is nothing in my mind! Samaya!"

In previous times, empowerment would not be given in public to large groups of people. Also, when empowerment is given to people who speak multiple languages, and there is no reliable translation for all attendees, there is some doubt whether all will effectively receive the empowerment. For an empowerment to be effective and meaningful, both the vajra master and the disciple must remain focused mindfully on the meaning of the words and the ritual. If this is not the case, we can only wonder whether it is beneficial. This is clear from the teachings of the masters. As Dudjom Rinpoche says,

> In previous times, when the profound meaning of empowerment was conferred, it was only for those who were certain to be able to practice and to maintain the samaya; there was no tradition of conferring it everywhere. There were true empowerments in which every word definitely carried symbolic meaning, and one definitely needed to contemplate its meaning; it is presumptuous to think otherwise, as if just having empowerment objects, such as the vase, touched to the crown of your head, tasting the water from the vase, and so on will ripen anyone's mind!

Similarly, Patrul Rinpoche admonishes,

> There are many teachers these days who practice the teachings without understanding them. By their base deeds, they ruin the Buddha's precious teachings, source of all benefit and bliss, from the foundations.

Receiving teachings from a guru based solely on their fame or high rank is just an exercise in blind faith. As stated in both the sutras and tantras, teachers and disciples must first examine each other carefully. It is important for us to follow this advice and genuinely investigate each other before giving or receiving empowerment. When the guru is examining the disciple, if they do not know the disciple's level, they should start with the sutra teachings and give tantric teachings gradually. If they know the disciple's level, they should—as Yukhok Chatral Chöying Rangdrol advises—give teachings accordingly.

Therefore, teachers who wish to benefit others should give profound Dharma teachings that are full of benefit and not dangerous, such as those on love, compassion, bodhichitta, the four thoughts, and so forth. If by doing so they reveal the path of what to adopt and what to abandon in accordance with karma, what could be more beneficial to living beings and the Buddha's teachings than that?

The power of the Vajrayana lies in the purity of the unbroken continuity of the lineage transmission from master to student. Before receiving empowerment, use your best judgment to examine the lineage of the teacher from whom you wish to receive empowerment and instruction. Develop an understanding of the lineage's teachings so as to develop your faith. Faith is the key that opens the door to the blessings of realization that are transmitted during an empowerment.

When there is an open connection between the teacher and the student, the transmission of enlightened realization is fresh, direct, and powerful. This type of enlightened wisdom, love, and power does not come from a book but from an unbroken living lineage. Therefore, to enter the Vajrayana and practice tantra, we must receive empowerment from a qualified guru, with a pure view and faith as our foundation.

Although we are never separate from our buddha nature, our primordial wisdom is temporarily obscured by ignorance. Just as ore is smelted to obtain pure gold, likewise, when the mind is ripened by empowerment, temporary delusion is clarified and original purity is revealed and recognized. Empowerment is a profound method to force transcendent wisdom to arise. Just as a strong wind swiftly disperses clouds to reveal an open sky, empowerment causes swift attainment of enlightenment by generating the profound tantric view and methods to realize buddhahood in this life, at death, or in the period between lives (bardo).

Even if rapid enlightenment is not possible, if the close bond between the vajra master and the student made during empowerment, the *samaya*, does not decline, one will eventually attain enlightenment based on keeping the pure samaya commitments. Therefore, it is important to know how to maintain the general root and secondary commitments of each of the four empowerments: (1) the vase empowerment, which purifies karmic obscurations; (2) the word empowerment, which purifies obscurations of negative emotions; (3) the secret empowerment, which purifies conceptual obscurations; and (4) the knowledge-wisdom empowerment, which purifies obscurations of habitual tendencies. When these four obscurations are purified, then one reaches enlightenment as a buddha. If this is done, then the Vajrayana will indeed become the supreme short path to enlightenment.

Two Causes and Four Conditions

You might ask, what conditions are needed to receive empowerment? How is the transcendent wisdom, which is the meaning of the empowerment, generated? How is the potential for transformation into the enlightened state placed in the mind? How can the correct causes be generated and problems be avoided?

In answer to these questions, Mipham Rinpoche specifies that two causes and four conditions must be complete to receive empowerment. The first cause, *concurrent similarity*, is the experience of great bliss simultaneous with the pure reality of dharmata pervading the disciple's channels, winds, drops, and mind. If one lacks the six elements—marrow, bone, and semen from the father's side; flesh, blood, and skin from the mother's side—one is not a qualified vessel for receiving empowerment. The second contributing cause is having all the ritual empowerment substances and implements consecrated and blessed by a qualified vajra master.

Regarding the four conditions, Mipham Rinpoche states that the first, the *causal condition*, is that the disciple must be a suitable vessel for empowerment, possessing renunciation, bodhichitta, confident faith in the profound meaning of tantra, and the aspiration to practice it correctly.

The second condition, the *possessed condition*, is the qualified vajra master whose mind has been ripened by a series of empowerments that is part of an unbroken stream of transmission and who has not transgressed the vows and commitments received during their empowerment. The vajra master's mind should be calm, with few negative emotions or concepts. They should have received signs of their own accomplishment by having had visions of the yidam deity through the approach and accomplishment practices.

The mind of the vajra master should have been liberated through realization of the ultimate mode of reality and filled with compassion—wishing to help others to obtain liberation. Having given up clinging to selfish desires for this life, the vajra master should be skilled in caring for disciples by whatever means necessary to train them. Having studied widely, they should be knowledgeable about the sutras and tantras, having practiced according to their lineage gurus' instructions. A guru possessing these qualities is the ideal and authentic vajra master.

While many qualifications of a guru are taught in the sutras and tantras, at minimum the vajra master must have love, compassion, and bodhichitta. They must have received empowerment from a qualified guru holding an unbroken lineage, have completed the retreat of the ritual to be given during the empowerment, and be skillful at conferring the empowerment ritual. A guru who practices in accordance with the Dharma and encourages others to practice in accordance with their lineage instructions is a qualified vajra master. When we meet such a guru, regardless of their outer appearance, we should rely upon them by pleasing them in three ways—offering practice, service, and material offerings—until we complete the conduct or practice in which they have instructed us. My root teacher, Khangsar Tenpe Wangchuk, says that students need to rely on their teacher until they have received all the necessary instructions—in other words, not just for a short period of time.

Third, the *immediately preceding condition* is that the stages of the empowerment ritual are conducted in the correct order. The earlier empowerments must be conferred before the later ones.

Fourth, the *object condition* is that the consecrated ritual objects, mantra, samadhi, mudras, and so forth are present without excess or omission. In particular, it is very important for the master and disciple to remain focused during the empowerment, contemplating the words and meaning with attention.

If all these causes and conditions are complete in the disciple and the vajra master, the time for tantric activity has arrived. When that happens, beings of the highest faculties will develop in their minds the special transcendent wisdom that is the meaning of the empowerment; those lacking the highest faculties will be endowed with the special potential to be suitable vessels ready to develop that wisdom.

In summary, having the complete set of two causes and four conditions is important. A Vajrayana practitioner who has these causes and conditions is a perfect vessel and suitable to receive tantric empowerment. If one attends an empowerment and these causes and conditions are not all present, the empowerment will not be received;

and furthermore, there are great faults. Those who are wise should be careful. To summarize:

> Don't confer empowerment without the two causes and four
>   conditions complete!
> Don't proclaim tantra to mass gatherings!
> Don't sell the teachings due to fame or greed!
> Don't trust charlatan practitioners!

12

Relationships

We have just examined the importance of the guru-disciple relationship that is forged during an empowerment and continues until one has accomplished the practice that the teacher has given the student. In the case of a vajra master and their student, this relationship may continue over lifetimes until enlightenment! Therefore, as a person who has been both a vajra master and a student of many great vajra masters, I have considered earnestly how to conduct myself and how to establish and maintain good relationships in my own life. Here I share some advice on relationships that has helped me and my students.

Relationships in modern life may be challenging, as our turbulent times make it difficult to control our emotions. Despite this, if we view our whole life as the path, then having relationships can enhance our life. They can be a source of joy and provide us with companionship during good times and bad. Relationships can teach us how to handle our own experiences. Sharing joy with others increases our pleasure, while sharing sadness can reduce our pain. When we are angry or ashamed, talking openly with someone whom we trust can help us relax and let go of those feelings. Learning how others solve their problems can give us hope that we can do the same thing. That's why relationships can be good for everyone. Of course, relationships can also make us feel uncomfortable when they are unhealthy. If we don't have a happy and harmonious relationship with our family or friends, then it is difficult to enjoy our life with them.

Having a good or bad relationship depends on how we relate to each other. If we wish to have reliable and trustworthy friends, we need to be that way ourselves. By practicing bodhichitta, we become good-natured, honest, and pure-minded. People who are short-tempered, jealous, or greedy never have good friends. Whoever we are, it is important that we not jump to conclusions but examine situations objectively. As Patrul Rinpoche says,

> Sentient beings have different convictions and karmic appearances. How could everyone have the same opinion of what is good and bad? In both Dharma and worldly affairs, there should be trust and consideration between people. Whoever we are, it is not possible that we are completely free of fault; therefore, it is said to be a mistake to be discourteous to some and consider them bad just because they have one fault while being polite to others and considering them good just because they have some good qualities.

How can we be a good friend? From a Buddhist point of view, harmony in every relationship depends on how much we control our ego—our self-centeredness. Think how wonderful it would be if we could enjoy our relationships with less attachment. We need to understand the difference between attachment and love. It is one of the Buddha's great kindnesses that he distinguishes between these two so clearly, because knowing the difference can save us from having unhealthy relationships. We can reduce attachment and increase love, which is guaranteed to bring us more joy.

When I first read about Milarepa, who abandoned his worldly life to focus only on attaining enlightenment, I felt that I could never be like him and do what he did. It harmed my confidence and gave me doubts about my capacity. I asked my teacher about my path versus Milarepa's. He told me that there is a way to attain enlightenment without needing to abandon worldly life. That was wonderful for me to hear as it gave me great confidence and enthusiasm. This could be beneficial for you to hear as well.

When we talk about practicing nonattachment in Buddhism, you might feel the same as I did and lose your confidence in your ability to generate true love. If you have a genuine motivation, then your attachment turns into unconditional love and your aversion turns into unconditional compassion. The difference between a relationship with true love and a relationship with attachment is that in a relationship with attachment, we care for others because we expect them to take care of us and give us something that we want or need. When we are attached to others, we have many expectations of them and don't see them for who they are. In reality, we are not caring for them, we are caring solely for ourselves.

I describe this type of love as fish love. If you say that you love fish, what usually happens? You eat it. So you see, you don't love the fish, you love yourself when you catch it, fillet it, fry it, and eat it. Therefore, a relationship based on attachment is similar to this fish love.

Buddhists say that attachment, anger, and ignorance all originate from the same family of the afflictions—and none of them are good for your relationships. If you have a sense of true love—not fish love—then there is genuine happiness and an opportunity for healthy relationships. When you understand that, you will feel relaxed and happy—this is the result of your true love. That is why I teach how important it is to have a bodhichitta mind and generate true love. Through your practice of these two, you will develop good relationships.

Try to avoid blaming others. If you want to communicate with your family or friends when you are upset, remember the mind training (*lojong*) slogan that advises us to drive all blame into ourselves. This will help you deal more skillfully with your situation. Usually when people are upset with their family or friends, the first thing their mind comes up with is that they didn't do anything wrong. They think the way to feel better is to prove that they are right and that the other is wrong. But it doesn't work like that. When you are arguing, you are not listening to each other, as your communication has broken down. The lojong teachings say that if you can accept the blame, then the situation will become much more workable, and you will be able to fix your problem. By accepting the blame, you open the door for communication to take place. This will be good for you and everyone involved to remember before striking out in anger. In the *Bodhicharyavatara*, Shantideva says,

> To cover all the earth with sheets of leather—
> where could such amounts of skin be found?
> But with leather soles just on my shoes
> it is as though I cover all the earth!

It is impossible to cover the whole world in leather to protect your feet, but you don't need to. You only need to cover your feet—and then it is as if the whole world is covered. When there is a problem, try to change yourself first. That is the best way to keep your relationships happy and healthy.

Jealousy

Jealousy is a big issue in relationships. The opposite of jealousy is rejoicing. First, when you are feeling jealous, investigate what is causing your jealousy. Let's pretend you are in a relationship and you see your partner getting along well with someone else. Often that gives you a feeling of jealousy. You want your partner's attention all for yourself because you only have fish love. Investigate your feeling of jealousy. Notice that you have feelings of attachment and you are jealous of your partner's attention. When you know exactly why you are jealous, then you can practice the antidote, which is letting go and rejoicing. Think of having true love for your partner. Rejoicing in your partner's happiness is the best antidote to your jealousy. It will reduce your attachment and increase your true love.

You can do this with any object of jealousy. Whatever you are jealous of, you can give it away and rejoice in seeing the happiness of the person who receives that object. If you have fish love, you will be jealous instead of happy. If you have true love, whenever your partner is happy, you will be happy. If you have decided that you want to build good relationships, be an open person who is honest and trusting. If your connection with other people is difficult, that means you are not open. If you cannot appreciate others and you are a jealous person, you cannot have good relationships. Try to be gentle with yourself, kind to others, and openly loving to the people in your life who wish to connect with you. Be grateful for all the people in your life.

Value your friendships and relationships by striving to develop your love and kindness. If you develop your love and kindness, then your mind will be loving. This is how you develop the causes of happy and healthy relationships. The Buddha said that when you show true love, in that moment, everyone is your friend. You must learn how to appreciate your relationships through the practice of loving-kindness and reducing your attachment. Attachment is all about me and what I can get from you; true love is all about what I can give you or do for you. In summary, to maintain your relationships, practice kindness, have fewer expectations, and blame others less for the temporary challenges that are bound to arise in life.

Loneliness

When you are lonely, you may have judgmental thoughts, such as *I don't have any friends to hang out with*. By judging yourself in this way, you develop your emotional discomfort, which makes the situation even more difficult. Letting go of such judgments will not take away all the pain of loneliness, but it will help you significantly.

Loneliness can be painful; therefore, how you deal with loneliness is important. Holidays or your birthday may be the most painful times because you may notice your loneliness more acutely. If you don't accept the loneliness, then you will continue to suffer. If you are frequently lonely, your difficulties in life will worsen and your joy will be minimized. If you already struggle with difficult emotions, loneliness can significantly increase your emotional distress. A good solution for loneliness is to make friends with others, meditate, read, and do other activities if you can. Most importantly, try to make friends with yourself. If you don't know how to live happily alone, then you are bound to suffer from loneliness.

I have learned to appreciate my time alone. I get to do whatever I want, whenever I want. I am the boss. Sometimes when I see other people fighting, it makes me feel very fortunate to be alone. When I do things by myself, it makes me feel strong and connected to myself. When I must accomplish things for myself, I appreciate all my capacities.

If you are feeling lonely, investigate if you can do more things by yourself and find happiness in those activities. Even if you have the chance to be with another person, it might be a good idea to build a connection with yourself and appreciate all the good qualities that you possess. If you do this, you will create a habit whereby you enjoy spending time just with yourself. Then you will be happy whether you are with others or by yourself.

If you have bodhichitta mind, you are connected to everyone. Therefore, mentally you are not alone or suffering from loneliness. If you are a spiritual practitioner, being able to be alone is an important skill to develop. Think of all the benefits of being alone—when you are alone, you have time to practice, listen to teachings and contemplate their meaning, read your Dharma books, and take care of your needs. Being alone can be good, as it can help you develop your wonderful qualities by giving you time to pursue your spiritual practices.

To summarize, I offer to you my "Prayer of Joyful Relationships." May you find it beneficial for your practice and your life.

PRAYER OF JOYFUL RELATIONSHIPS

May all beings have happiness and increase their peace of
mind.
May all beings let their love flow throughout the entire
universe.
May all beings find contentment within their relationships.
May all beings be free from suffering loneliness and be filled
with joy.

May I be a luminous light for those who have lost their way in
darkness.
May I be a source of love and peace for all relationships
encountering difficulty.
May I be an excellent bridge for those who need a connection.
May I be a best friend for those who need companionship.

May all beings' relationships progress peacefully; may their
friendships flourish continually.

May all beings' relationships grow harmoniously; may their
love bloom unconditionally.

If I have hurt anyone, knowingly or unknowingly, I ask for
their forgiveness.

If anyone has hurt me, knowingly or unknowingly, I extend
my forgiveness.

Let us pray for harmony in the sangha and work together
with unity and love.

Let us extend that harmony throughout the world and share
all our blessings.

Let us dedicate ourselves to the well-being of others and live
together as brothers and sisters.

Let us attain enlightenment together in this very life and
dispel the suffering of the world.

OṂ ŚĀNTI ŚĀNTI MAHĀŚĀNTI SVĀHĀ

PART TWO

Preparing for Birth, Death, and the Bardo

How Mind Comes into Being

If we do not understand our mind, there is no way to attain true happiness or dispel suffering. Therefore, it is important to learn about the nature of our mind during this precious human life. This point is clearly explained in Buddhist scriptures. The manner of presentation of mind in sutra and tantra differs according to the needs of trainees; however, ultimately both express the same idea.

Matter and Consciousness

All beings and the environment come into existence interdependently; they arise within subtle continuums of being from the element of space. From a Buddhist point of view, before this world arose, there was only emptiness. Within this emptiness, a very subtle stream of substance brought forth the entities of our world and its beings through a process of dependent origination. This is the only way beings and environments are produced. Otherwise we would have to accept that they arise without cause or from a creator—neither of which is possible. This is an extensive topic, and for interested readers, the Middle Way school of philosophy discusses these arguments in great detail.

From this philosophical reasoning, our body and mind arise dependent on their causes, and their substances are extremely subtle continuums that, if finely analyzed, are seen to be without beginning or end. Thus, examining the continuum of the form aggregate in this way, we see that although there is no beginning or end to form as such, the form continuum of this particular life does have a beginning and end.

Why is it that some instances of this extremely subtle continuum act as the cause for matter alone, while others act as the cause for mind and awareness? This can be understood by reflecting on the different reactions that arise when scientists combine various chemicals. Different combinations have the potential to produce various gases, liquids, and solids.

Change occurs depending upon the force of physical causes and conditions that come together. For example, if salt is added to a bowl of water, a salty taste arises; whereas if a sweet or sour substance is added, those tastes arise. Another traditional analogy is the *utpala*, a blue lotus flower that blooms in various ways depending upon the contributing conditions that are present. Or consider how forests and leaves that existed long ago are petrified rock today through the force of physical change. It is obvious that changes in the external world happen in dependence upon the transformation of physical substances.

Internal changes are subtler than changes in the external world. The existence of various atoms and their different forces and potentials has been clearly defined in the Buddhist scriptures. Khenchen Tsultrim Lodrö summarizes:

Particles have three aspects. First, the gross appearances occur when particles affect each other; these are the visual forms, sounds, and so forth that appear to us during our life. Second, when the grosser aspect is broken down into smaller, subtler parts, everything exists as the nature of atoms. Like particles of dust that appear in the sunlight, things exist only as particles that do not contact each other, gathered in the empty sky at the same moment. Beautiful and ugly forms, sweet and unpleasant sounds, and so forth, arise from causes; the atoms do not possess beauty or ugliness. They are not even seen by our ordinary eyes. The third aspect is that particles are the nature of empty space, without the slightest existence of their own. In the context of subtle particles merely arising within this space-like empty nature, the aspects of form, sound, and so forth do not exist in the slightest. Still, out of that emptiness, through the force of interdependence, particles once again merely appear. Just this is the basis or source of the world's composition; there is nothing else that can withstand logical analysis.

Clarity and Cognition

What is the difference between matter and consciousness? Simply put, matter is without clarity and cognition, whereas consciousness has these. With its clarity and cognition, our mind can know all things with certainty and is able to understand objects correctly. We can see the vivid, multicolored appearances of objects around us without needing to consult anyone else. Any being that has clarity and cognition has a mind with the same desire to experience happiness and avoid suffering as we do.

Clarity and cognition arise from the previous moment of our mind's continuum, and the present moment's clarity and cognition are the cause of the next moment of mind. Because we have consciousness in every moment, it is impossible that we could ever be without it; therefore, our mind is a continuum without beginning or end. Indeed, the Buddha, with his transcendent wisdom, said he could not see a beginning or end of consciousness. We should understand that the Buddha's *not seeing* accords with the ultimate mode of the nature of mind, the perfect truth seen by omniscient wisdom that is unimpeded in its knowledge of all phenomena.

Buddhist scriptures explain that although one sentient being possesses both subtle and gross levels of mind, their consciousness is unitary. Yet outwardly they appear to have different functions, expressions, and potencies, as if there were many different consciousnesses. In the scriptures on valid cognition (*pramana*), the example is given of a lamp placed in the middle of a house with different colored windows. Even though there is only one lamp inside the house, because of the windows there appear to be multiple lamps shining with various colors of light, when you look at them from outside the house.

The multiple sense consciousnesses arise in dependence upon many causes and conditions, including the various parts of the brain and the nervous system. For example, for perception of form to take place, the object, sense organ, and mental consciousness must come together in the first moment. In the second moment, consciousness is generated in the aspect of the object. In the third moment, the entire subject-object relationship has been established.

Many gross levels of consciousness depend upon our body. They exist as long as we have our body; when our body is destroyed, they cease to exist. For example, feelings that arise in the mind, scents that arise when smelled by the nose, and tactile sensations experienced by the body can all be clearly recognized by one or another part of our brain and will cease when the brain ceases. However, the connection between our brain's function and our mind is only temporary. Given their different natures, how could it ever be established that the brain and our consciousness are one and the same? It cannot, yet most neuroscientists and philosophers of the mind think that the brain and our consciousness are one. This is no doubt the basis of their belief that past and future lives do not exist.

The power of the mind is immeasurable and inconceivable: even if someone understood the brain and all its functioning, they still would not be able to correctly understand the characteristics of consciousness. Khenchen Tsultrim Lodrö says,

> For example, when tears flow from someone's eyes, their expression changes. As they sob, we directly see and hear the tears and sound of their crying. Even instruments can detect movement in the brain as well. That is all, however.
>
> The inner experience, the suffering of a being parted from a friend, compassion felt for other living beings, special experiences of joy, and so forth can only be known by the person who is weeping; it is as if others have no way of experiencing it.

Furthermore, as noted, there are many different levels of refinement in consciousness, from gross to extremely subtle. The extremely subtle level of consciousness is known only through the meditative experience of yogins and yoginis; it could never be understood just as it is by scientific instruments. Many people identify body and mind as a single entity, possessing the same causes and conditions. If this were so, the mind would have to be an adventitious phenomenon, just like the body; when the body disintegrates, the mind would have to cease as well. This mistaken belief leads to disregarding reincarnation and karmic cause and effect; as a result, people have acted and continue to act badly in whatever way they wish, as if there is no virtue or vice.

13

How Birth and Death Occur

When any being takes rebirth, their consciousness enters the middle of the union of the egg and sperm. The main cause for coming into existence is the undamaged sperm and egg of the parents with the power to conceive. As simultaneous contributing conditions, there must also be full capacity of the five elements. In dependence upon the potency of the sperm, egg, and the five elements, the embryo gradually matures through the various stages of development until it is born from the womb. The way the body is produced through the meeting of the sperm and egg, and so forth, is explained in generally similar ways by Buddhists and scientists.

Our present body came from the sperm and egg of our parents. As we have seen, however, our consciousness does not. Since consciousness is a momentary, uninterrupted continuum of clarity and knowing, there is absolutely no way that the unknowing physical body could be its substantial cause. Whenever the causes and conditions are complete, the bardo or intermediate-state being will enter and be conceived within a realm that corresponds to the projection of their mind. Therefore, when the causes are all present, even if the result is unwished for, there is no stopping its production.

For indeterminate lengths of time, bardo beings experience continual sufferings of various types until the causes and conditions for the creation of a body are complete for them to take rebirth. The process by which karma ripens is inconceivable and incalculable; therefore, there is no certainty with regard to the type of body one may take. In Buddhist philosophy, there are traditionally six realms that correspond to six emotions and their resulting bodies. These are the god realm (pride), demigod realm (jealousy), human realm (desire), animal realm (ignorance), hungry ghost realm (miserliness), and hell realm (anger). A person may take birth as an animal, an animal may take rebirth in hell, a hell being may take rebirth as a hungry ghost, and so on. Beings discard various bodies to take up all sorts of other bodies.

In general, a living being's body comes into existence from the individual's various karmic causes and conditions that they have created to produce it. How then, after they die, could a living being possibly reincarnate just as they wish? As I mentioned above, they cannot. Their rebirth depends upon the karma that they have created in their previous life and the causes and conditions that exist at the time of death. If the causes and conditions come together for them to be born into the human realm, they will be reborn in our realm. Otherwise they will go to another realm and be unable to return to ours at that time.

Many Western people have misunderstandings about karma. As explained previously, in general, *karma* means "action." Everything that we experience is the result of our actions—we create the causes by our actions and we experience their results. We reap as we sow: whatever quality of action we engage in, its corresponding result will follow without fail. Therefore, the results of our karmic actions must be deposited into the continuum of consciousness. As explained before, consciousness is without beginning or end. Many people do not believe this view and have ridiculed it. Still, it is important not to waver in our belief in this profound teaching of cause and effect. We should not ignore or neglect it.

Although there are many ways for the body and mind to come into being, they can be summarized in four ways: birth from heat and moisture, miraculous birth, birth from an egg, and womb birth. There are, for example, many causes and conditions for womb birth; however, there are three main ones: the sperm of the father, the egg of the mother, and the consciousness of the intermediate-state or bardo being. It is easy to understand how the living being's body comes into existence from the joining of the egg and sperm, but that is not enough. The egg and sperm must join with something that is hidden to our ordinary perception: the consciousness of an intermediate-state being. When we die, our five elements dissolve into one another, all our gross consciousnesses cease, and we faint into the *alayavijnana*, the all-ground consciousness or mind basis of all, which will be discussed shortly.

The Dissolution of the Elements

It is helpful to offer a brief explanation of the dissolution of the elements. When a living being is born, they are born in dependence on the five elements: earth, water, fire, wind, and space. As long as they are alive, they live in dependence on these five elements. Finally, at the time of death these elements dissolve, one into the next. At the conclusion of this dissolution process, our life ends, our body and mind separate, and the mind moves on. Even before death, our elements deteriorate as we age, dissolving at the end into the basis from which they arose before. As *Great Awareness Itself Appearing* states,

> *Kye!* Friends! When beings' breath runs out, the external five
> elements dissolve into the internal five elements, the internal

five elements dissolve into the secret five elements, and the secret five elements dissolve into the perfected five elements.

Earth Dissolving into Water

As the five elements become unbalanced and dissolve one into the next, signs appear. Due to the form aggregate dissolving, for example, the power of the earth element declines and becomes unable to serve as the support for the consciousness associated with the earth element. This is called *earth dissolving into water*.

A sign that this is happening is that the body loses its strength and feels heavy, as if it were sinking into the earth. The brightness of the body is lost, the legs become thinner, residue accumulates on the teeth, one cannot spit or blow the nose, and so forth.

At the same time, the eye sense power dissolves. The eyes sink into the skull and become unable to move. Outer appearances are no longer seen clearly. All of these accompany the decline of the form aggregate.

Water Dissolving into Fire

As for dissolution of the sensation aggregate, at this point, the power of the water element declines and becomes unable to support the consciousness of the water element. This is called *water dissolving into fire*. A sign of it is that the moisture in the body dries up. For instance, nasal mucus dries up; and no smell, taste, or feeling is experienced. With dissolution of the ear sense power, no external or internal sound is heard. All this accompanies the decline of the sensation aggregate.

Fire Dissolving into Wind

Next the aggregate of perception dissolves. At this time, the power of the fire element, along with its related factors, declines and is lost. This is called *fire dissolving into wind*. A sign of this is that the body heat decreases and is finally lost altogether. Because awareness flickers in and out of clarity, a person cannot recognize their relatives and friends. As the fire element dissolves, food is no longer digested. As the nose sense power dissolves, the upper energy winds slowly dissolve.

Wind Dissolving into Space

Then the aggregate of karmic formation dissolves. At this time, the power of the wind element declines and becomes unable to support its corresponding consciousness. This is called *wind dissolving into space*. Its sign is that the inner and outer breath cannot move properly; the dying person experiences long exhalations, difficult inhalation, and finally the cessation of breath. The clarity of the voice declines until vocal expression of every sort ceases. Because the tongue sense power is dissolving, the tongue becomes thick, short, and blue.

Cognition becomes deluded—various pure and impure perceptions appear. At this point the heart stops and the external breath ceases. With the cessation of all the gross awarenesses—visual, audial, olfactory, and gustatory—the dying person becomes unable to apprehend objects of sight, sound, smell, and taste. Although the outer breath has ceased at this time, mental consciousness still remains in the body. There are many levels of subtlety to this mental consciousness.

In short, because of the decline of the sense organs that are the basis for the gross, nonconceptual sense consciousnesses, all the consciousnesses related to them cease and dissolve into the mental consciousness. Mental consciousness gradually ceases and dissolves into the alayavijnana.

The Three Appearances

When all concepts have ceased, the outer sign is that all appearances become like pure space, free of clouds and pervaded by moonlight;

this is called the *white appearance*. The sign of the next stage is similar: like a pure cloudless sky pervaded by sunlight; this is called the *red appearance*. Then consciousness faints away; the outer sign is that of a sky pervaded by dense blackness, called the *black appearance*.

These three appearances arise to most ordinary beings at death but extremely briefly, not remaining for more than a moment. Then all dualistic appearances, even those of these three appearances, dissolve into a state of clear light, free of all projections. At that time, the outer sign of this stage is a vision of a cloudless sky of brilliant clarity, without center or limits. It is said that the inner appearance is nothing but nonconceptual, transcendent wisdom, free of all projections that appears for an instant.

In the tantric systems of Dzogchen, it is said that the actual clear light of the ground appears; if at that time we recognize our own face, our true nature, we perceive the actual clear light. It is further said that consciousness dissolves into the clear-light mind that is the clear light of the ground. This is the final clear-light mind, as taught in the tantras, that follows the three dissolution-process appearances of white, red, and black.

The Meeting of the Mother and Child Clear Lights

If we have been well trained in the path of clear light through practicing Dzogchen meditation, it is said that we will naturally recognize our nature of mind at the time of death. This is described as being like a child jumping into a mother's lap, a river meeting the ocean, or the meeting of old friends, because having been introduced to the clear-light nature of mind before, you become a buddha in that instant!

To explain, the mother clear light is the transcendent wisdom that is primordially intrinsic to ourselves—the ground clear light. When our guru introduces us to this and we meditate on it, that is the path clear light, which is like a child. When these two, the mother and child, are unified, that is called *the meeting of the mother and child clear lights.*

Longchenpa says that when consciousness dissolves into clear light as explained above, even if someone is an ordinary being, from the point of view of their gross and subtle conceptual thought having ceased, and dualistic obscuration being absent, they are no different from the buddhas. Buddhas, however, through the force of having completed training on the path, have forever abandoned dualistic thought completely, such that it will not arise again; whereas for ordinary living beings, the clear light appears for an instant, but because they have not trained on the path and have not abandoned the imprints of white, red, and black appearances, dualistic thought and concepts will arise again.

The master Ngawang Chöpal Gyatso (Lochen Dharmashri) says that the ground clear light is the primordially pure dharmakaya intrinsic to all sentient beings. When we meditate on the points of the oral instructions revealed to us by our kind guru and become familiar with the child clear light, then mix this with the ground clear light at the time of death, our abiding in that state of nonconceptual, transcendent wisdom is the meeting of the mother and child clear lights. Thereby we are enlightened instantly. Lochen Dharmashri states that another way of saying this is that at death we are liberated in the dharmakaya clear light; this primordially pure dharmakaya is enlightenment itself.

Therefore, instant enlightenment is not really instant. People who spend their whole lives practicing well recognize clear light, the nature of their mind, at the time of death because of their diligent practice of their guru's instructions. They can remain in the death meditation known as *tukdam* for a week or more, as they wish. When the mother and child clear lights are unified after death, that meeting is the mind of luminosity, which we call *tukdam*. *Tuk* means "mind"; *dam* has many meanings, however, in this context it means "secret" in reference to the secret mind or luminosity. This luminosity is the deepest level of consciousness or the subtlest mind. Tukdam is a post-mortem state in which the body stays fresh for a week or more without decomposing, even though the heart and breath have stopped. During this time, the person is still in meditation, which prevents the body from decaying. When the meditator leaves tukdam, a sign of that is the emergence of the white and red bodhichitta drops from the deceased person's nostrils. I have personally seen this after some great practitioners' death meditations.

For advanced meditators like this, at the conclusion of tukdam, the energy of transcendent wisdom causes their awareness to exit from the crown of their head and they attain enlightenment. An ordinary being does not recognize this self-arisen clear-light awareness and its appearance ceases. Then the aggregate of consciousness reemerges out of the five aggregates. All one's karma, delusions, and habitual patterns arise, and one is born into the mental body of a bardo being to wander between death and rebirth until it is time for the next life.

The Alayavijnana

As I mentioned before, when the mental consciousness gradually ceases, it dissolves into the alayavijnana. What is this alayavijnana? There is disagreement among the Buddhist scriptures on this subject; however, because it is important to understand this term, I will explain it briefly. The Tibetan word for alayavijnana is *kunshyi namshe*, which means the "mind basis of all" or the "store-consciousness." It is the ground for the six consciousnesses; the seventh, or afflicted, consciousness; the fifty mental factors; and the eighty indicative conceptions—all our various emotional and cognitive states. Thus, all phenomena emerge from this consciousness as a consequence of these seeds or imprints. Yukhok Chatral Chöying Rangdrol states,

The alaya is like a vessel that accumulates all our previous thoughts and that acts as a foundation for the proliferation of future thoughts. The alaya does not have thoughts, so it is like space free of clouds. Since it holds the imprints of previous awareness and is the foundation of future thought, its nature is profound and extremely subtle.

The term *alaya* is defined in two ways, depending on the context in which it is used. One definition is the "primordial nature of mind"; another is the "obscured basis of impure phenomena." The first alaya has always existed, and it is the basis of all uncontaminated phenomena, the ground from which all pure forms and transcendent wisdom appear. The second alaya is impure, the basis of samsara and of all contaminated phenomena. The great Nyingma master Longchenpa explains,

> When we are calling someone, and our awareness is neutral and not thinking of anything for a moment, if what appears does not cease but remains clear and vivid—without grasping or conceiving anything—that aspect of clarity and nonconceptuality is the alayavijnana.

Similarly, Nyakla Pema Dündul says that when someone has been running with a heavy load and stops in the middle of a meadow to rest, their discursive thought ceases. That nonconceptuality is the alayavijnana. From that mind basis of all, the five sense consciousnesses develop; from that emerges conceptual thought, and from that arises disturbed, deluded, and afflicted mind states. However, all these states of consciousness are one at their base.

The reason for this is that if nonconceptual awareness, such as visual awareness perceiving an external form, was a different substance from the conceptual awareness that examines that form—and decides whether it is beautiful or not—it would absurdly follow that a person's mind would be hidden from themselves—as what is seen by one type of consciousness would not be experienced with awareness. Mipham Rinpoche says the alayavijnana is like the ocean and the various consciousnesses are like its waves, arising and subsiding in the ocean.

First, to reinforce, the alayavijnana is merely clear cognitive awareness that does not fall into any bias whatsoever; second, it is said that it observes the entirety of beings and the environment; third, it is unclear in aspect; and fourth, it is the support for all karmic imprints and propensities.

The alaya is said to be very difficult to understand. So I will explain more about the definitions of alaya. This manner of explanation comes from my extensive experience in studying the Buddhist scriptures. I had a great opportunity to study the alaya consciousness from four different traditions of Tibetan Buddhist philosophy and follow the commentarial tradition of each guru's oral instructions.

First, when we say the alaya is mere clarity and cognition without bias, we refer to the clarity and cognition that pervades all consciousness, from the visual through the mental in equal measure. For example, gold pervades gold earrings, bracelets, and necklaces; although their appearance and shape are entirely different, they are all similar in being gold. Likewise, the visual, audial, and other consciousnesses are completely different in characteristics and ways of grasping their objects, but they are all similar in being clear and cognizing. What is being posited here is that clarity and cognition pervades all awareness yet is not biased toward any of them.

Second, the alaya is said to observe the entirety of the environment and the beings within it. It does not observe just some objects, as visual consciousness observes only visual form or audial consciousness perceives only sound; rather, it pervades all objects without falling into any category. From the point of view of its being clear awareness, it is said to observe the entire environment and all beings equally. This does not mean that there is some other consciousness that, after peeling away all the various forms one by one, will be found observing all beings and the environment. Continuing the metaphor above, once you remove all the gold earrings, bracelets, and necklaces, there is no more gold to be found.

Third, the alaya is said to be unclear in aspect. This does not refer to the lack of clarity involved when an infant or an older person lacks clarity in looking at a visual form. Nor does it mean the lack of clarity of a conceptual thought apprehending its object by way of a generic image, as opposed to the clarity of direct perception that apprehends its object's specific characteristics. Rather, it means that it does not distinguish individual outlines or parameters of objects but observes all objects in general. In this sense, it is said to be a mind that observes the vast environment and beings yet without being clear.

Fourth, it is said to be the base for all karmic propensities and imprints. The various appearances of happiness and pain occur in the mind and arise through the power of the mind. The operation of karmic cause and effect, functioning in connection with inner awareness, is said to be unfailing. All the imprints of our good and bad karma from beginningless time accumulate upon our mind and eventually give rise to various appearances, such as those of the present. These imprints of different karmas can only be placed within consciousness, not matter, because the continuum of our physical form will cease at death, and karmic imprints continue from life to life. Also, physical matter has no ability to bear the imprints of karma because, as we have seen, it is not clear and cognizant; only mind is.

Therefore, among the many different consciousnesses, the alayavijnana is the consciousness upon which the imprints of good and bad karma are placed. It could not be the same as, for example, visual or audial consciousness because we have those consciousnesses at times, but at other times, as when we are blind or deaf, we do not. If imprints were placed upon visual consciousness, they would go to waste and not be able to mature. Furthermore, since visual consciousness is biased toward one type of object, it is unsuitable to act as a basis for the appearance of *all* external and internal things.

Therefore, all imprints of virtuous and unvirtuous karma that have been created in connection with visual and other consciousnesses are said to accumulate in the alayavijnana. When an action's potential or propensity to produce a later effect has not ripened, it remains in the nature of a seed. When that karmic seed ripens, it appears as various places, bodies, and experiences. These various appearances of karmic imprints do not exist in truth—they merely appear like a dream.

14

Existence in the Bardo

After death what arises is the intermediate state known as the *bardo of becoming*. The Tibetan words *sipa bardo* have been translated in various ways. *Sipa* means "possible," "becoming"—which means this life is a continuation of samsaric becoming—or "temporal" because life is changeable and impermanent. Therefore, it's temporary. Sipa bardo also refers to beings who have a mind in the intermediate state, which is simply the interval between any two states. For example, right now, this very moment that we experience is in between past and future. According to Buddhism, this moment is the most important moment that we have. What we do and how we handle this moment is all that matters.

So, there are different ways to explain the meaning of sipa bardo, but here the meaning is the period when this life's appearances have subsided and the future body has not yet been taken, during which many pleasant and painful feelings are experienced. Therefore, it is called the *intermediate* or *in-between existence between death and birth*.

In general, the bardo teachings can be taught in many different ways. Usually the bardos are divided into four (or six): the *natural bardo of this life*, the *painful bardo of dying*, the *luminous bardo of ultimate nature*, and the *karmic bardo of becoming*. For our purposes, a brief introduction to the karmic bardo of becoming will suffice.

During the period when the habitual tendencies and mental appearances of the previous body are mostly past and the habitual tendencies for the mental appearances of the future life have not yet arisen, there is a mental body of the in-between state that moves on, experiencing various hallucinations within the bardo of becoming.

During the bardo of becoming, the mind doesn't have a physical support. There is only a subtle light body, like a form reflected in water. The imprints of previous grasping at the true existence of the body result in the continuous appearance of a mental body that resembles a distorted reflection in water. As it is a clear, bright body, it can move without impediment through objects as large as mountains or as small as the eye of a needle.

The two gates through which it cannot pass are the mother's womb and Vajrasana, the vajra seat in Bodhgaya where the Buddha attained enlightenment. These two gates are not literal places. According to Lochen Dharmashri, the vajra seat symbolizes nirvana, the nature of the immutable inner sphere of Bodhgaya, where all the buddhas attain enlightenment; the mother's womb symbolizes any impure birthplace in the six realms of samsara.

Because the consciousness of the bardo being lacks a gross physical base, it can arrive instantly anywhere it wishes, wherever it directs its aspiration. The bardo being, therefore, does not remain in one place. Like a feather carried away by the wind, the bardo being is light and flies through space weightlessly.

Its body has no shadow. With an appearance like that of a submerged form reflected in water, the bardo being is tormented by fear and suffering. When the texts that introduce the bardo are read to someone recently deceased, there are signs that they are told to realize in order to recognize that they are wandering in the bardo with a consciousness that has separated from a physical body. Due to holding on to previous negative imprints, a person may not recognize that they have died. Although they approach and speak to members of their family or friends, when their beloveds don't see, hear, or answer them, the bardo being experiences intense suffering due to attachment, anger, and delusion.

It is said in the bardo instructions that for up to three and a half days, the body, land, home, property, friends, and relatives of their previous life appear to the bardo being, but as soon as that threshold is past, flickering images of the body of their future life appear. When the bardo being sees that others are enjoying their house, wealth, property, and so forth, it makes that bardo being extremely angry or filled with regret, thus, creating incredible hallucinations of suffering.

Since the bardo mental body has no fixed place, bardo beings roam through empty houses, caves, valleys, in space, and so on. Because they have no fixed conduct, they do anything whatsoever, as all their appearances are unstable and momentary. There is no certainty of sustenance; they are unable to enjoy food unless it is dedicated to them with blessings of mantra, ritual, and samadhi. With the uncertainties of the mental body, the various appearances experienced by the bardo being do not stand up to analysis; they arise one moment, then cease as other appearances arise. When the latter appearances arise, the previous ones disappear and are forgotten. Thus, varied experiences of happiness and suffering occur.

If we have died, it is important to check whether these signs are appearing to us. If they are, we are in the bardo, and it is important for us to remember the bardo instructions and to recognize the state. Having recognized that we are in the bardo, it is vital to turn our aspiration toward virtue. The gurus say that in the bardo, it is important to not only aspire to virtue but also understand the ultimate nature of reality and the instructions for the intermediate state.

Not only do the bardo appearances lack true reality—so do our own present external appearances—but they are no different from experiencing terror in a dream. Determining that all appearances are deceptive in this way and by practicing the profound bardo instructions without attachment to any appearance, we may attain enlightenment now or in the bardo. At all times, in every situation, it is important to maintain the aspiration to be free from attachment.

The bardo body changes very easily. As the consciousness is very clear, it is deceived by even subtle thoughts. However, it is said that even an instant of insight into the lack of inherent existence of phenomena can liberate us. This is good news. Therefore, these good, bad, and neutral appearances are *mere appearances* that arise through the force of mind now and in the bardo. We must recognize this. If our mind changes, our external appearances change. According to the Buddha's teachings, the various appearances change just by the power of mind, and they lack any inherent existence separate from mind. It is an indisputable, perfect teaching.

When two people practice in different ways, they will have different feelings and experiences. For example, if harmonious friends go to a garden and talk about how they feel about a beautiful flower, even though the same flower appears to their eye consciousness, they will have different thoughts and feelings about it.

In a similar way, Milarepa was once seen lying naked on a path by two young girls in Dingri in Tibet. The girls saw his emaciated body and prayed that they would never take birth in such a green-tinged body. Milarepa said to the girls, "You need not worry! You won't be born in a body like mine even if you pray for it!" For someone like Milarepa, whatever he experienced was a cause for the increase of his pure visions and joyful bliss. He experienced appearances of bliss throughout the day and night, sang songs of realization, and constantly poured out Dharma instructions like clouds of blessings. He had inconceivable realized qualities, such as being unhindered by his thoughts, because he recognized the equal taste of bliss and suffering—the equality of all phenomena.

We can understand from the examples above that all inner and outer phenomena are ultimately only our mind. It is said that as long as we cling to appearances as truly existent, we will never be able to train in the bardo. The gurus say that whatever terrifying appearances arise to us now, it is very important to decide with certainty that they are our own mind. It is especially important to remain undisturbed and continuously practice what we know will help us to accomplish our aspirations. Due to the different karmic appearances of bardo beings, they will experience happiness and suffering differently. However, for most sentient beings, the appearances of the bardo of becoming will arise as described above, after the five elements dissolve at death.

The Life Span of a Bardo Being

The life span of a being in the bardo is extremely uncertain. It is said in the introduction to the bardo teachings that, in general, beings remain forty-nine days in the bardo. However, some stay many months and years without a physical embodiment. Some, if the conducive conditions arise, take embodiment after just a few days. Some remain in the bardo for even shorter periods of time or do not experience the bardo of becoming at all. For example, when the ground clear light appears, special beings endowed with supreme realization merge the mother and child clear lights into one and are enlightened in that very moment.

In contrast, unvirtuous beings—those with the worst karma—experience the intense suffering of lower rebirth the very moment their breath ceases. They go down to hellish states without any bardo existence or intervening rebirth of any kind.

Furthermore, yogins and yoginis with supreme realization perform *phowa*, the transference of consciousness, to direct their consciousness wherever they wish and therefore do not experience the bardo of becoming. Someone who takes rebirth as a god in a formless realm does not experience the bardo of becoming as they possess a formless meditation body of samadhi.

Apart from these exceptions, as explained above, all sentient beings who die experience a bardo existence of indeterminate duration and with various appearances. Bereft of free will about where they will go, they experience suffering. The root of these appearances of happiness and suffering is karma and delusion. They arise because our mind, which is the root of all, is out of control. The *Saddharmasmrityupasthanasutra* says,

> The mind's our enemy, our mighty foe;
> no enemy exists apart from this our mind.
> Like tinder burned by flames itself has kindled,
> the mind is scorched and burned by mind itself.

All karmic appearances, all experiences of happiness and suffering, arise through the force of our pure and impure intentions, our states of mind. Like appearances in a dream, they appear without existing in reality and cause us to experience strong feelings, like terror, despite being merely dreamlike illusions.

For example, if you put one hand in hot water, your other hand in cold water, and then place both together in body-temperature water, the hand that was in the hot water will experience cold, whereas the hand that was in the cold water will experience heat. Both experiences are just mentally experienced feelings; they are not truly existent external realities of temperature.

Therefore, statements such as "Negative karma causes us to take rebirth in bad realms of existence and suffer" should be understood in a similar light. As Shantideva explains in the *Bodhicharyavatara*,

> The hellish instruments to torture living beings—
> who invented them for such intent?

Who has forged this burning iron ground;
whence have all these demon-women sprung?

All are but the offspring of the sinful mind,
the mighty Sage has said.
Throughout the triple world therefore
there is no greater bane than mind itself.

Otherwise, I don't think places such as hells in other worlds externally exist. Buddhist scriptures, however, speak of many world systems in other dimensions, as well as living beings in those world systems with different karmic appearances. Who can say with certainty, therefore, that worlds of impure karma, such as hell, definitely do not exist? There is no need to doubt, however, that the different karmic appearances of bliss and pain are not externally existent objects. They arise solely dependent on the power of our mind.

To return to the many bardo beings, it is said that the number of bardo beings is inconceivable, and that all of them are distraught because they have only a mental body. They put great effort and hope into their search for a physical body, the way a person tormented by extreme thirst looks for a drink of water. Finding no place to go, they can't stay still. As they ride their wind energy, they pass their time in fear and sadness, and they wander until they find a place to take rebirth.

This is similar to a person who leaves their homeland behind forever and is subjected to various sufferings on the treacherous journey until at last they reach their destination. That, in general, is the experience of the bardo beings. It is very beneficial for you, while alive, to meditate on the potential experiences of the bardo to prepare yourself. If you meditate now, it will be easier to recognize the appearance of the bardo, and your liberation will be more immediate.

The teachings on the bardo are good for people who think about this life and their future lives. For Buddhists, every moment of our life and between lives is considered a bardo or moment of transition. For example, right now we are in the natural bardo of this life that began at our birth and will end with our death. After we pass away, we will find ourselves in another bardo. Therefore, whether or not you are Buddhist, it is important to study the bardo teachings, as each of the six has its own unique instructions and meditation practices. (See the teachings on Karma Lingpa and the six bardos on my YouTube channel.)

For example, in the natural bardo of this life, we talk about how to take care of ourselves and live a meaningful life by developing bodhichitta and eliminating our ignorance. Because of our habitual misunderstanding of these mere appearances as real, we cause ourselves suffering. Ignorance causes the idea of a dualistic world, which leads to ego-clinging; ego-clinging leads to the rest of the afflictions, such as anger, attachment, pride, and jealousy.

In Tibetan, ego-clinging is called *dak dzin*, which also can be translated as "self-grasping." As long as we have the ignorance that grasps at the self, we are suffering in samsara. Therefore, we need to find a way to eliminate this ignorant self-grasping. As practitioners of Buddhism in this life, we have the opportunity to transform our ignorance about the nature of appearances by bringing our experiences onto the path of enlightenment. While we are human and fortunate to have a body that supports our mind, we need to take advantage of this situation and develop the qualities of love and compassion. What is the essence of life? It is love and compassion.

The bardo of this life is the most important bardo because everything that happens afterward depends on the bardo of this life. The most important thing we can do in the bardo of this life is to have genuine bodhichitta. At the very least, we should enter the path of the Dharma. People are always interested in what they should do in the bardo after death, but if they don't practice now, it will be difficult then; indeed, it will be too late. The other five bardos depend on this bardo. If you have good results in your practice now, you won't need to worry about experiencing the other bardos.

Even if you don't want to practice but just live an ordinary life, it is important to remember now how to live correctly in this bardo. Generally we have an outer life and an inner life; the inner life is spiritual development. To be successful in the inner life, we must practice the teachings.

We should think carefully about how many years have already passed since we were born and how many years remain. Death can happen at any time; we need to remember that our lives are impermanent. If we remember this, it helps us to practice and motivates us to do so diligently. The *Mahaparinirvanasutra* states,

> Of all the footprints, that of the elephant is supreme. Similarly, of all mindfulness meditation, that on death is supreme.

Because awareness of death increases our commitment to spiritual practice, if we have the habit of practicing during this life, it will be easier to practice when we pass away. Therefore, my root teacher Khenchen Jigme Phuntsok always said that we should contemplate that death is inevitable, that the time of death is uncertain, and that our lives are impermanent and very fragile. There are two main causes of death: either our time has run out or an accident causes our death. Death is a part of our lives and it will certainly happen. At the time of death, a peaceful mind is very important, whether or not you are Buddhist.

At the moment of death, we should try not to feel anger, attachment, or any other negative emotions. It is better to pass away in a peaceful manner. Dharma practitioners have different experiences in the bardos whether they are great practitioners, middling practitioners, or lesser practitioners. The way each type of practitioner dies and how they experience the bardo depends upon their ability as a practitioner during their lifetime.

What Happens after Death?

Western society has a limited understanding of what happens in the process of death and what happens after death. Although many religious traditions accept rebirth, from my own experience, many Westerners may not be comfortable with the concept of sentient beings coming to this present life from their previous lives and taking rebirth after death.

Some religious traditions accept that past and future lives exist, and they believe in rebirth based on faith alone, without any reason. Others view past and future lives as caused by a creator. Some say that if certain deeds are not performed, their creator will be displeased, and they will take rebirth in hell. There are many such concepts that are without foundation. In the *Description of Past and Future Lives—the Lamp of Existence*, Khenchen Tsultrim Lodrö says,

> In the early system of Christianity, reincarnation was
> accepted. But later a Roman emperor was afraid that if it
> was taught, it would harm the effectiveness of imperial rule.
> Therefore, he consciously deceived his subjects by teaching
> that after death a person could not take rebirth as a human
> being (or other forms) but only in heaven or hell.

In Buddhism, however, the existence of past and future lives is affirmed, and it is considered important to recognize this fact during our present life. As Buddhists, we assert that through the force of karma, body and mind temporarily come together in a relationship of mutual dependence, but we do not assert them to be the same essence or entity.

Body is *lu* in Tibetan, which means something to "leave behind." When we die, we must leave our body behind. When the body disintegrates, consciousness does not cease to exist; therefore, we assert the existence of future lives. As noted, it is taught that consciousness—

hence, samsara—lacks both beginning and end, and thus it is impossible to posit the number of times that any sentient being has taken rebirth.

As a metaphor, if we were to count how many juniper berry–sized balls of soil could be made from the entire earth, at some point, we would run out of soil; but there is no end to counting the previous rebirths of any living being. The presentation of past and future lives is without doubt a true depiction of the actual nature of our existence—not stories made up by children. Both Buddhist scriptures and modern scholars give various reasons for the reality of reincarnation.

The Proof of Reincarnation

In our era, many neuroscientists assert that consciousness is merely a temporary side effect of the brain that ceases with the death of the brain, thus denying that reincarnation is possible. Why this is wrong must be addressed. There is an argument for the reality of reincarnation. It is that people remember past lives. Some people remember past lives because of the unique makeup of the subtle channels and elements of their body or through the force of their karma. Some yogins and yoginis remember their past lives through the power of their meditation.

There is no reason to doubt past lives just because we ourselves don't remember them. You may not clearly remember what you dreamed last night or what you said or did yesterday. Yet you trust the existence of your past experiences from yesterday, even if you don't remember everything fully.

Yogins and yoginis report through the power of their unbroken awareness that the first moment of this life is preceded by the last moment at death of the mind of the previous life. The mind is a continuum of consciousness; therefore, our memories—whether of yesterday or our previous lives—are a continuum, a storehouse of our karma. Many people have extremely credible memories of past lives that, unless we simply deny the veracity of their experience, we cannot deny the reality of what they describe.

Dr. Jim B. Tucker, a prominent psychiatrist and researcher who heads the University of Virginia's Division of Perceptual Studies, was one of the first Western university professors to study these memories of previous lives in depth, and he published the results in his book *Life Before Life: Children's Memories of Previous Lives*. Over the years, his team has rigorously studied thousands of cases and presented this research to the scientific community and the general public to demonstrate the extraordinary statements made by children that are beyond coincidence.

One example is the case of Patrick Christenson. He was born in Michigan in 1991, and immediately after giving birth, his mother felt a connection to a previous child, Kevin, who had died of cancer over ten years before. Remarkably, Patrick had three markings on his body that matched markings on Kevin. At the age of four, Patrick began recalling memories of Kevin's life. He described surgery that Kevin had undergone and where it had occurred on his body. He also told his mother he wanted to go to his old home, the house where he had left her. He described the house as a black and orange house, which were the same colors as the house where Kevin lived. Kevin's pictures were not normally displayed in the house, but when one was seen by Patrick, he said that the picture was a picture of himself.

Thousands of similar cases were investigated and documented by Dr. Tucker and his research partner and teacher, Dr. Ian Stevenson. Neither are Buddhist practitioners, nor do they accept the veracity of reincarnation on faith, but they have been collecting evidence to determine the most logical and well-supported explanations based on their scientific views.

If you were going to disprove the existence of past and future lives, you would have to do it using three logical reasons: First, you would have to show that your consciousness had no existence before the egg and sperm of your mother and father met—in other words, you would need to prove that your mind did not exist prior to your birth. Second, you would have to show that your consciousness did not come from a previous place or time. Third, you would have to be sure that your consciousness stems only from your brain and body. Absent these three, you cannot disprove the existence of past and future lives. As Khenchen Tsultrim Lodrö states,

> Thinking or saying that you cease to exist after you die is the speculation of someone who has no idea about the secrets of life. It does not make use of correct logic; we should be very careful about this. It is not suitable to be completely ignorant of crucial facets of our lives, such as birth and death.

If we check objectively, without bias, it is difficult to avoid accepting these proofs.

Why Previous Lives Are Not Remembered

If past lives exist, why do some people remember them but most people don't? While yogins and yoginis remember their past lives through the power of compassion, prayers, and through wisdom arising from meditation, some remember past lives through the force of their karma. Children most likely remember their past lives more than adults. It is easier for a child to recall recent memories from their previous life. If they were an adult at the time of death, they will commonly recall their husband, wife, or children; and if they were a child at the time of death, they will more commonly talk about their parents and siblings. Many children remember their past lives if their death was more violent, sudden, or painful. The age of six or seven is when some children stop talking about a previous life as that is the same age when they lose most of their early childhood memories.

The reason most ordinary beings don't remember their past lives as they go through the process of death, intermediate state, and rebirth is that at the time of death, when all the grosser sense consciousnesses cease and dissolve into the alayavijnana, the ability to remember deteriorates. At that time, we fall into a faint similar to that of deep sleep. When that state clears, most sentient beings see the varied appearances of the bardo between death and rebirth.

Lacking a gross body, the bardo being has an empty form made of consciousness itself, an unobstructed mental body. If all the causes and conditions for entering a womb are not complete, it remains in that state. When all the causes and conditions are complete, then multiple indeterminate appearances arise through the force of karma, and a sentient being may enter a womb and take rebirth. At this time, when a living being has discarded its previous body and found the physical form of its next rebirth, the channels, winds, and drops form anew, and the activities of the former life are forgotten. In Buddhist scriptures this is called *obscurations of the womb*.

When people fall unconscious suddenly, they don't remember their previous activities. If people can forget their prior activities after only a short period of unconsciousness—when they regain consciousness in the same body with the same channels, winds, and drops—then they certainly won't remember their previous life after all their gross consciousnesses have ceased and they have taken rebirth in a new body with new aggregates and elements. To summarize:

Even without omniscience knowing past, present, and future,
I have enough courage to analyze hidden things—
and enough confidence to say:
past and future lives exist.

15

Instructions for the Time of Death

When the dissolution of the elements described before occurs, we should not let our mind wander toward anything else but stay focused firmly on contemplating the impermanence of all compounded phenomena, in particular the uncertainty of the time and the cause of our own death. We should remember our guru's instructions to not be attached to anything, including our friends, family, and loved ones.

It is very important to mentally purify and renounce all harmful acts that we have committed during our life. With as much mindfulness and alertness as we can muster, we should meditate without distraction. This enables us, in our future life, to remember imprints and various facets of our past life. For instance, if we set our mental alarm clock for a certain time in the morning with mindfulness and alertness, we can awaken exactly at that time. Fundamentally it is extremely important for us to die with an undisturbed, peaceful, and happy state of mind.

The process of dissolution described previously is the way it usually occurs, but it is not completely certain; it is said there are other ways that it may occur. Because of the differences in living beings' channels, winds, and element drops; because of conditions caused by sickness, spirits, or sudden death and so forth, the process of dissolution may proceed differently. Therefore, it is extremely important to know the process of dissolution as explained and to continually familiarize our mind with it by meditating upon it.

Whether someone is a spiritually advanced being or an ordinary being, it is very important that the body not be moved when they die but be left untouched for at least three days. As has been described, a person with advanced ability to meditate remains in clear light and enters tukdam meditation. If their body is moved, it will disturb their meditation, and this would be extremely unfortunate.

For their part, ordinary beings sometimes are unable to leave their body due to attachment. Others are unable to die quickly due to the conditions of their disease, and their subtle consciousness remains in their body for a number of days. Therefore, if their body is quickly moved or destroyed, one incurs the fault of causing them extreme suffering, almost as if one had killed them.

Ordinary beings should, if at all possible, die lying on their right side. If the person dying is a Buddhist, say the names of the buddhas and their mantras into their ear and place on their tongue blessed Dharma medicine. Before my father passed away, in accordance with his wishes, we performed the hundred peaceful and wrathful deities empowerments for him; he told me it was the most powerful ritual he had ever received.

It is powerfully beneficial for a dying person to be shown tantric mandalas and to have ablution rituals and empowerments conferred upon them. In short, in the wake of death, no matter how much virtue is accomplished on their behalf, it is extremely important that it not be mixed with nonvirtue of any kind.

At the moment of death, as I mentioned before, we should try to not feel anger, hatred, or other negative emotions. It is better to pass away in a peaceful manner. If the time comes when we can no longer practice actively, the only really important thing to do is relax, stay calm, and rest in the nature of mind as much as possible. It doesn't matter whether our body or brain is still functioning—the nature of our mind is always present. There is nothing new that we need to learn or understand. We should just be natural and let go of everything. If we have done virtuous things, especially in this lifetime, we should remember to dedicate the merit to benefit all living beings.

GUIDED MEDITATION ON THE BARDO

In general, all the hallucinations of the bardo are nothing but appearances of our own mind, so we can use our mind to transform them into whatever we wish. To prepare for this during life, we should practice transforming all appearances into pure appearances, both during the daytime and when we dream at night. This is done by viewing all appearances as the guru's body and mandala; all sounds as the guru's voice and the mantric resounding of the Dharma; and all thoughts as the guru's self-arisen transcendent wisdom, the state of primordially pure dharmakaya. The great treasure revealer Karma Lingpa states,

> Now when the bardo of death appears to me, I will abandon all grasping and attachment. Enter into the nature of the clear oral instructions without distraction. Transfer my consciousness into the unborn space of self-arising awareness. As I am about to leave this compound body of flesh and blood, I will know it to be a transitory illusion.

At the time of death, we may become overwhelmed by feelings of sadness, fear, pain, and regret because of our attachment to the appearances of this life. If we can let go of our grasping, then this bardo is no longer the *painful* bardo of dying. We should meditate by settling our mind in its natural state without thought and free of fabrication.

By reflecting repeatedly that our body and all appearances are mere reflections of our mind and that these reflexive appearances are not truly existent, we can release all impure, deceptive appearances into the expanse of pure, transcendent wisdom.

In short, there are three important practices for dying. Ideally, you should rest in the nature of your mind and generate bodhichitta. If you can't do either of these two, then I encourage you to ask for the blessings of the enlightened beings by practicing aspiration prayers that arouse your pure devotion to your lineage and trust in the efficacy of their teachings on bodhichitta—the union of wisdom and compassion—to guide you toward enlightenment.

PHOWA

Another bardo instruction is that of phowa, the transference of consciousness. Phowa is a useful practice when, at the time of death, our mind and body start to separate and lose their connection. It is described as the *ejection of consciousness*, the practice of *conscious dying*, or as achieving *enlightenment without meditation*. Milarepa says that phowa is a path that can be practiced by those who lack experience or who are not highly skilled at meditation.

There are five different kinds of transference of consciousness. First, there is the superior transference to the dharmakaya.

The dharmakaya transference is for people who have developed and established stability with recognizing the nature of their mind and their natural state so that at the moment of death, they can practice Dzogchen, the union of emptiness and appearance, and transfer their consciousness into the dharmakaya. Dharmakaya transference is a formless practice and therefore does not use any visualization. This is the best form of phowa because there is an immediate transference of consciousness from the state of confusion into the wisdom nature of mind. At the time of death, you simply rest without distraction in the natural state.

Second, there is the middling transference to the sambhogakaya, which is accomplished through the union of the generation and perfection stages of the Vajrayana. The sambhogakaya transference is for people who are familiar with practicing the generation and perfection stages in union. They are trained in seeing the yidam deity as a magical appearance. Because of this, when the hallucinations of the intermediate state arise at the time of death, they can transfer their consciousness into the sambhogakaya. Sambhogakaya transference is based on the deity yoga—the yidam practices—of the Vajrayana. When we can clearly visualize ourselves in the form of the yidam deity and that experience is stabilized as the realization of the purity of appearances, then we are engaged in the practice of Vajrayana phowa.

Third, there is the lower transference to the nirmanakaya that is achieved through great compassion. The nirmanakaya transference is for people who have received the empowerments of the Secret Mantrayana; have perfect samaya commitments and enjoy practicing the generation and perfection stages; and have received instructions on the intermediate state. Those who practice this transference must block any unwanted entry into an impure womb. With bodhichitta, great compassion, and applying the practice of taking rebirth as a nirmanakaya emanation, they transfer their consciousness toward rebirth in one of the buddha realms.

Fourth, there is the ordinary transference using the three recognitions—the recognition of our central channel as the path; recognition of our consciousness as the traveler; and recognition of the environment of a buddha realm as the destination. Ordinary transference is for people who practice phowa by imagining the central channel as the path, the *bindu* of mind consciousness as the traveler, and a pure realm of great bliss as the destination.

That is why this type of transference is called the *three metaphors or recognitions*—it has the metaphor of the path, the traveler, and the destination. It is also related to the nirmanakaya transference because you transfer your consciousness into the nirmanakaya manifestation of Buddha Amitabha's compassion. The ordinary transference of the three recognitions is the phowa practice most often done by ordinary beings and is therefore the method commonly associated with these teachings. It uses a more detailed form of visualization than the other methods.

And finally, fifth, there is the phowa performed for the dead with the guru's hook of compassion. The hook-of-compassion transference is done either for a being near death or already in the intermediate state. It can be performed by a yogin or yogini with realization and the ability to recognize the consciousness of a being in the intermediate state. Nonetheless, anyone who has some experience of the phowa instructions on transference of consciousness and knows unmistakenly the right moment to perform it—which is when the outer breath has stopped but the inner breath still continues—can perform it at that very moment. If a spiritual friend points out the correct path to take, it is extremely helpful for the dying person as this instruction has the potential to prevent rebirth in the lower realms.

How to Practice Phowa

To practice phowa, follow these instructions:

Visualize yourself as Vajrayogini, a female meditational deity who symbolizes the indestructible nature of mind, or, if you prefer, visualize yourself in your ordinary body. Visualize your central channel in the very middle of Vajrayogini's or your body. The central channel is vivid, bright blue in color, insubstantial, and straight. As it is the pathway to liberation and higher rebirths, it is open at the top. It is closed at the bottom, four fingers below the navel, symbolizing that all access to samsara and lower rebirths is blocked and sealed.

In the central channel at the heart center is a green sphere of light, a tiklé. Sitting just above this tiklé is the red seed syllable ༄ (HRĪḤ), the essence of your consciousness. Focus clearly on this seed syllable and merge your mind with it inseparably. Above your head, visualize Amitabha, the buddha of boundless light, who embodies all the buddhas.

The ritual for ejecting your consciousness starts as you recite HRĪḤ, HRĪḤ, HRĪḤ, HRĪḤ, HRĪḤ. Visualize that your consciousness, in the form of the red seed syllable HRĪḤ, is lifted upward by the light-green tiklé as it rises higher and higher. As this tiklé emerges from the crown chakra at the top of your head, simultaneously cry out *hik!*, turn your eyes sharply up, and visualize the tiklé shooting up and dissolving into Buddha Amitabha's heart.

At the end of your phowa session, seal your practice in the expanse of the dharmakaya by saying PHAṬ—ཕཊ! Rest in the natural state for some time; thereafter, Buddha Amitabha dissolves into light and into you.

There are two parts to practicing phowa: first, the training we do during our lives; second, the actual practice at the time of death. During our life when all our body's channels, energies, and essences are intact and energetic, we will find that performing the transference is quite difficult. However, once we arrive at our final hour, or in extreme old age, it becomes much easier. It is like fruit on a tree—it is hard to pick while it is still growing. However, once it is ripe, it falls off the branch with the slightest touch.

The time to put phowa into actual practice is after the signs of approaching death have already appeared—when you are sure that there is no turning back and the process of dissolution has already begun. Do not practice the actual transference at any other time than this because it could be very dangerous. The difference is our motivation. Right now our motivation is training in phowa. We don't really wish to die, as it is not our time. During the actual transference at the time of death, our motivation is a genuine one. We wish to transfer our consciousness—that is the difference.

You may ask, *How can I use this practice to help someone who is dying?* The view and the practice are exactly the same; the only difference is that you visualize the aspects of the practice happening within the central channel of the dying person. In addition, you visualize Buddha Amitabha above the head of the dying person. Do the phowa practice and visualize that the rays of light descend into the dying person, purifying their negative karma. Their consciousness dissolves into light and merges into Buddha Amitabha.

If you are doing this practice as you are approaching death, sit as comfortably as you can. Feel that you are undoubtedly in the presence of the buddha who is for you the quintessence of the truth, wisdom, and compassion of all the buddhas, masters, and enlightened beings merged into one. Fill your heart with your chosen buddha's presence and trust that they are inseparable from you.

In brief, this is how we do the visualization and recitation for phowa practice according to the Nyingma lineage. By practicing in this way, we are preparing to eject our consciousness at the moment of death and merge it with the wisdom mind of the Buddha—what Padmasambhava calls the space of unborn awareness of rigpa. Phowa is a yogic meditation practice that has been used for centuries to prepare for death and to help those who are dying. I hope that you will benefit from these instructions.

Wherever we take rebirth in the three realms of samsara, we are not beyond suffering; therefore, we shouldn't be attached to that rebirth. Samsara arises from karma, which arises from delusion. If we do not abandon delusion, we will not be liberated from samsara. If we wander in samsara, there is no end to suffering. Thinking along these lines, meditate repeatedly on being disillusioned with samsara and practice renunciation, resolving to definitely go toward liberation.

In the introduction to the bardo teachings, there are instructions that we should meditate on in order to close the door of the womb. The gurus instruct us to repeatedly pray to take rebirth in a perfect body with leisure and endowments, powerfully able to serve the Dharma teachings and benefit all sentient beings—and to be able to swiftly attain enlightenment in that very body.

CONCLUSION

In all times and situations, we should be—as Patrul Rinpoche advises—gentle and kind, satisfied and content with our share, and self-sufficient—examining things skillfully while being honest and altruistic toward all.

Thus, we can live our life in accordance with what is harmonious and profoundly helpful for ourselves and others. My sincere wish is that you will devote your life toward generating bodhichitta through the methods shared in this book on the heart of life. By training your mind, by being sincere and having pure intentions, you will have few desires and may cultivate great love and compassion for all.

As I mentioned above, if we cultivate these essential qualities, no matter what happens, we will be happy and easygoing. Even while remaining in impure realms of existence, we will enjoy the inconceivable bliss and happiness of our buddha nature, and our joyful presence will be a blessing to everyone.

Through the virtuous merit of these instructions, may all beings develop the qualities of bodhichitta and realize the bliss of enlightenment.

ACKNOWLEDGMENTS

I would like to acknowledge from my heart, with the most profound gratitude, all my lineage teachers—especially my five root teachers—who gave me the nectar of the Dharma and who were such beautiful examples of how to live a meaningful life filled with bodhichitta. I am grateful for Cortland Dahl, who first gave me the opportunity to come to the United States to teach, along with everyone at Bodhicitta Sangha | Heart of Enlightenment Institute who continues to support my life and Dharma activities. I would like to thank Kate Thomas for editing this book and creating the glossary; Roger Jackson for his comments, suggestions, and sharing the wisdom of his experience; and Kelly O'Neil for helping me write the biographies of my root teachers. Finally, I appreciate the entire team at Shambhala Publications for helping this book be published in such a beautiful way. I freely admit and confess to any mistakes within this book.

Khenpo Sherab Sangpo

GLOSSARY

This glossary includes the main names, places, and terms mentioned in the book. The phoneticized version of Sanskrit and Tibetan names is given, with Sanskrit transliterations according to the International Alphabet of Sanskrit Transliteration (IAST) scheme in parentheses.

Adzom Drukpa Thupten Padma Trinle (1926–2001). One of Khenpo Sherab Sangpo's five root teachers, he was the reincarnation of Adzom Drukpa Drodul Pawo Dorje (1842–1924), an important master in the Dzogchen lineage.

alayavijnana (Skt. ālayavijñāna). The all-ground consciousness is the fundamental clarity and cognitive capacity of the mind that is the subtle basis for all conscious experience. This mere clarity and knowing is the support for all habitual tendencies and, therefore, it is often metaphorically described as a storehouse where the karmic traces of past actions are stored as seeds that can ripen into future experience.

Ananda (Skt. Ānanda). One of Buddha Shakyamuni's foremost hearer disciples (*arhat*) who was also his cousin and attendant; he memorized the sutras—the oral teachings of the Buddha—and these discourses became part of the three collections of teachings called the Tripitaka.

Atisha Dipamkara Shrijnana (Skt. Atiśa Dīpaṃkara Śrījñāna, 982–1054). A great Indian master and scholar who spent the last ten years of his life teaching and translating texts in Tibet. His disciples founded the Kadampa school of Tibetan Buddhism.

atman (Skt. ātman). A permanent unitary self that is asserted by non-Buddhists to exist independently from other phenomena.

bardo (Skt. antarābhava). A Tibetan word that indicates a transitional period in between two states—such as the natural bardo of life that occurs during the period between birth and death.

bhumi (Skt. bhūmi). A stage along the Buddhist path of practice. As a practitioner progresses through each level, their enlightened qualities increase with each bhumi that they accomplish.

Bodhgaya (Skt. Bodhgayā). Location of Vajrasana (Skt. Vajrāsana), the vajra seat, where under the bodhi tree Buddha Shakyamuni attained enlightenment.

***Bodhicharyavatara* (Skt. *Bodhicaryāvatāra*).** Commonly translated as *The Way of the Bodhisattva*. Shantideva's (685–763) guide to the Mahayana bodhisattva path according to the Nalanda (Skt. Nālandā) tradition of Indian Buddhism.

bodhichitta (Skt. bodhicitta). Commonly translated as "enlightenment mind." *Bodhi* means "enlightened" or "awake"; *chitta* means "heart" or "mind."

bodhisattva. Someone who has generated bodhichitta and wishes to bring all beings to the state of enlightenment.

Bötrul Dongak Tenpe Nyima (1900–1959). A great Nyingma master who was the direct disciple of Khenpo Kunzang Palden Rinpoche, the close disciple and biographer of Patrul Rinpoche. Böpa Tulku, as he was also known, upheld the lineage of Mipham Rinpoche and was the root teacher of Khenchen Padma Tsewang and Khenchen Chöying Chapdal, two of Khenpo Sherab Sangpo's root teachers.

buddha nature. According to Mipham Rinpoche, buddha nature is naturally present as a potential in all living beings as the essence of the nature of their mind. It is because of this potential that all beings are capable of attaining enlightenment.

Buddha Shakyamuni (Skt. Śākyamuni). The great sage (*muni*) of the ancient Shakya (Skt. Śākya) kingdom in India and founder of the Buddhist path. He was born in the sixth century before the Common Era, renounced his life as a royal prince, and attained enlightenment.

Buddhadharma (Skt. Buddhadharma). The teachings of Buddha Shakyamuni. See *Dharma*.

Chandrakirti (Skt. Candrakīrti). A philosopher born in the seventh century in India who was, like Shantideva, a renowned follower of the Prasangika Madhyamika (Skt. Prāsaṅgika Mādhyamika). This philosophical approach was first established by the Indian scholar Buddhapalita (Skt. Buddhapālita) and then expanded upon by Chandrakirti in his work *Introduction to the Middle Way* (*Madhyamakāvatāra*). The main approach of this philosophical tradition is to apply consequentialist arguments to establish the ultimate truth of emptiness beyond all conceptual elaboration. In the Nyingma lineage of Mipham Rinpoche, followers of the Prasangika Madhyamika are defined as those who teach by emphasizing the uncategorized absolute that is free from all assertions.

deity yoga. See *yidam deity*.

dependent arising (pratityasamutpada [Skt. pratītyasamutpāda]). The key insight of Buddha Shakyamuni upon his awakening was that all phenomena arise in dependence upon causes and conditions. When Shariputra, one of Buddha Shakyamuni's foremost hearer disciples, asked for the essence of the teachings, the reply was the teaching on dependent arising. This essence was transmitted by its dharani, which was given by Lord Buddha directly to Ashvajit (Skt. Aśvajit), who was one of the first five disciples to have received the teaching on the four noble truths at Deer Park. The *Pratityasamutpadahridaya* dharani is memorized and recited by Buddhists to this day:

OṂ YE DHARMA HETU PRABHAVĀ HETUN TEṢĀṂ
TATHĀGATO HY AVADAT TEṢĀṂ CA YO NIRODHA EVAṂ
VĀDĪ MAHĀŚRAMAṆAḤ SVĀHĀ
　OṂ, the Tathagata proclaimed the cause of those phenomena that arise from causes, as well as their cessation—thus taught the Mahashramana, SVĀHĀ.

Dharma. A Sanskrit word that has ten primary meanings that range from knowable phenomenon to spiritual traditions in general, according to Vasubandhu, a fourth-century Indian scholar who composed the *Abhidharmakosha*. In this book, Khenpo Sherab Sangpo primarily refers to the Dharma as the teachings of Buddha Shakyamuni.

dharmakaya (Skt. dharmakāya). The truth body of a buddha. As a key term in Dzogchen, the dharmakaya is the primordial wisdom that is indicated by the guru during the pointing-out instructions on the nature of mind. Additionally, Karma Lingpa's bardo instructions define the dharmakaya as the clear light of the unborn space of self-arising awareness that can be recognized by a practitioner to accomplish the dharmakaya phowa transference at death.

dharmata (Skt. dharmatā). The innate or ultimate nature (suchness) of phenomena and mind.

Dodrupchen Jigme Tenpe Nyima (1865–1926). A respected Nyingma master born in eastern Tibet whose father was Dudjom Lingpa. He received many teachings from great masters—Patrul Rinpoche, Jamyang Khyentse Wangpo, and Mipham Rinpoche, among many others—and wrote many works, including two commentaries on the *Guhyagarbha Tantra*.

Dromtönpa (1004–1064). A great bodhisattva and the main Tibetan disciple of Atisha Dipamkara Shrijnana. He transmitted the teachings on mind training (Tib. *lojong*) to Potowa Rinchen Sal, who in turn transmitted them to the two known as the sun and moon of Ü—Sharawa Yönten Drak, who possessed the wisdom of the Dharma; and Langthangpa Dorje Senge, who had mastery over bodhichitta. Khenpo Sherab Sangpo's root teachers, especially Khenchen Jigme Phuntsok, placed great emphasis on teaching Dromtönpa's and the Kadampa masters' curriculum of mind training.

Dudjom Lingpa (1835–1904). The treasure revealer who discovered the *Zabsang Khandro Nyingtik*, one of the four main cycles of treasure (Tib. *terma*) revealed in 1862, from several treasure sites in eastern Tibet. This cycle of practice includes the preliminary practice, *The Chariot of Liberation*, that Khangsar Tenpe Wangchuk asked Khenpo Sherab Sangpo to give to his students as a foundation for receiving Dzogchen teachings. Dudjom Lingpa's immediate reincarnation was Dudjom Rinpoche (1904–1987), a great master and author of *The Nyingma School of Tibetan Buddhism: Its Fundamentals and History*.

Dzogchen. A contraction of two Tibetan words: *dzogpa*, which means "complete" or "perfect"; and *chenpo*, which means "great." The Dzogchen teachings comprise the atiyoga yana (Skt. *atiyoga yāna*), the ninth vehicle in the nine yanas classification system of the Buddhist path according to the Nyingma lineage that was founded by Padmasambhava during the eighth century in Tibet.

eight ordinary siddhis. Eight temporary accomplishments that arise from the yogic discipline of spiritual practice. The supreme or uncommon siddhi is the attainment of buddhahood or enlightenment itself.

four noble truths (Skt. catvāryasatyāni). After Buddha Shakyamuni attained enlightenment, he taught the four noble truths to his first five disciples in Deer Park. The truth of suffering, the truth of the origin of suffering, the truth of cessation, and the truth of the path are foundational teachings in Buddhism.

Garab Dorje. The first human master of the Dzogchen lineage, who gave his last testament to his disciple Manjushrimitra (Skt. Mañjuśrīmitra) in three statements called *Tsik Sum Né Dek*. The three statements that strike the vital point are:

Introducing directly the face of rigpa itself.
Deciding upon one thing and one thing only.
Confidence directly in the liberation of rising thoughts.

Gendun Chöphel (1903–1951). A Tibetan teacher, poet, traveler, and author of the great philosophical work *Clarifying the Core of Madhyamaka: Ornament of the Thought of Nāgārjuna*.

Geshe Chekawa Yeshe Dorje (1101–1175). A Kadampa master who composed *The Seven Points of Mind Training*.

Hinayana (Skt. Hīnayāna). A word for a path of Buddhist practice that is often translated as the "lesser vehicle," in contrast to the "greater vehicle" of the Mahayana. According to Thich Nhat Hanh, at the time when the Buddha's discourses were written down in Pali (Pāli), there were a total of eighteen or twenty ancient schools of Buddhism. The sole surviving school is known as Theravada (Theravāda).

homage (Skt. namo). A word from the French language. *Namo guru*, or "homage to the guru," indicates showing respect for the buddhas, bodhisattvas, and lineage teachers who inspire and guide a student on the path toward enlightenment.

Jamgön Kongtrul Lodrö Taye (1813–1899). A student of Jamyang Khyentse Wangpo and the teacher of Mipham Rinpoche, who composed and edited the ninety-volume collection of texts called *The Five Great Treasures.*

Jigme Lingpa (1730–1798). A great teacher, scholar, author, and treasure revealer who discovered the Longchen Nyingtik cycle of teachings and practices through a series of visions of the great fourteenth-century master Longchenpa.

Kamalashila (Skt. Kamalaśīla, 740–795). An Indian master and scholar of the ancient monastic university of Nalanda, who is known for his three texts called *Stages of Meditation.*

karma. A Sanskrit word that means action. Each action has a cause that results in a similar effect. If the cause is positive, then happiness results. If the cause is negative, then suffering results. Each action and its result can be classified as virtuous, unwholesome, or neutral karma.

Karma Lingpa (1326–1386). The fourteenth-century Nyingma treasure revealer of *The Root Verses on the Six Bardos* from the Zabchö Shitro Gongpa Rangdrol cycle of terma teachings. This cycle contains the teachings that are known to Westerners as the *Tibetan Book of the Dead.*

Khenchen Chöying Chapdal (1920–1997). One of Khenpo Sherab Sangpo's root teachers who studied twelve years with Bötrul Dongak Tenpe Nyima—who recognized him as the reincarnation of Rongzom Chökyi Zangpo (Rongzompa). He lived a simple life of renunciation and yogic discipline. Like Milarepa, he practiced *chulen* (*rasayana* [Skt. *rasāyana*]), the alchemy of extracting essences, and survived periods of hardship during the Cultural Revolution on very little food. His dedication to teaching up to the day he died was critical to the revival of Tibetan Buddhism after 1959.

Khenchen Jigme Phuntsok (1933–2004). A great Dzogchen master who was Khenpo Sherab Sangpo's second root teacher. He founded Sêrta Larung Gar in Kham in eastern Tibet in 1980, one of the largest Buddhist teaching centers in the world. Mumé Yeshe Tsomo, his niece, and Khenpo Tsultrim Lodrö are some of the main teachers who continue to guide the institute today.

Khenchen Padma Tsewang (1931–2002). A great scholar, bodhisattva, and enlightened being who was Khenpo Sherab Sangpo's first root teacher and a spiritual father to him. He reestablished the monastic curriculum and taught at Pukang, Shechen, and Dzogchen monasteries, thereby playing a great role in the revitalization of Buddhism in Tibet after the Cultural Revolution.

Khunu Lama Tenzin Gyaltsen (1895–1977). A great bodhisattva, Sanskrit teacher, and author of *Vast as the Heavens, Deep as the Sea: Verses in Praise of Bodhichitta*, who held the lineage of Patrul Rinpoche's teachings on Shantideva's *Bodhicharyavatara*.

lojong. The Tibetan name for the Buddhist mind training teachings that were brought from India to Tibet by Atisha in the eleventh century.

lung (Skt. prāṇa). The Tibetan word for the inner air or wind energies within the subtle body that flow through the channels and affect how the senses and other bodily functions operate.

mahamudra (Skt. mahāmudrā). A Sanskrit term that can refer to the ultimate fruition or the path of practice that results in the supreme spiritual accomplishment of the Kagyü lineage which passed from Maitripa and Naropa in India to Marpa Lotsawa in Tibet.

mahasandhi (Skt. mahāsaṅdhi). A Sanskrit term which means great gathering. The mahasandhi teachings are often referred to as Dzogchen teachings within the Tibetan Buddhist context.

mahasiddhas (Skt. mahāsiddhā). Great adepts who attain accomplishments (siddhis) through their spiritual practice. The most famous of these are the eighty-four mahasiddhas of India.

Mahayana (Skt. Mahāyāna). Commonly translated as the "greater vehicle" or "universal vehicle," a Buddhist path whose teachings center on shunyata (emptiness)—the absence of inherent existence in all phenomena—as explained by the Buddha in the sutras of the second turning of the wheel of the Dharma and further elaborated upon by philosophers, such as Nagarjuna and Chandrakirti.

mandala (Skt. maṇḍala). A circular diagram—painted on cloth, made from colored sand, or a metal plate for offering grain—that symbolizes the universe of a yidam deity surrounded by his or her retinue, palace, and sacred environment. The mandala offering, during which one symbolically offers the entire universe to a field of merit, is performed before receiving

Vajrayana teachings and accumulated as part of the preliminary practices to generate merit and wisdom by practicing unconditional generosity.

Mantrayana (Skt. Mantrayāna). See *Vajrayana*.

marigpa. A Tibetan term that means not knowing or ignorance. In the context of Dzogchen, it means not recognizing the view of the dharmakaya nature of mind.

Middle Way. The teachings of Buddha Shakyamuni that avoid the two extremes of eternalism and nihilism.

mudra (Skt. mudrā). A sacred hand gesture performed during Vajrayana rituals. Mantra, mudra, and samadhi are performed together to respectively evoke the enlightened speech, body, and mind of the yidam deities and their retinues.

Nagarjuna (Skt. Nāgārjuna, 150–250). One of the six great ornaments or commentators on the Buddha's teachings; he is respected as an unsurpassed master by all Buddhist schools. His teachings provide the foundation for the Madhyamika that propounds the highest view of the Middle Way school of philosophy. He was also the revealer of the prajnaparamita (Skt. prajñāpāramitā), the core teaching of the second turning of the wheel of the Dharma on the perfection of wisdom.

Ngawang Chöpal Gyatso (1654–1717). The younger brother of Rigdzin Terdak Lingpa, the founder of Mindroling Monastery, an important center for Nyingma teachings established in 1676. He was known as Lochen Dharmashri as he was a great translator and scholar who wrote important commentaries on the *Guhyagarbha Tantra*.

nirmanakaya (Skt. nirmāṇakāya). A Sanskrit term that means the form body of a totally and completely awakened buddha who manifests to benefit others.

nirvana (Skt. nirvāṇa). The state of liberation that an arhat achieves when his or her mind is purified and free from afflictions.

Nyakla Pema Dündul (1816–1872). A student of the great Dzogchen master Do Khyentse Yeshe Dorje and founder of Kalzang Monastery.

Nyingma. Known as the Early Translation or Nyingma school in Tibetan; the lineage of Padmasambhava, the great tantric guru and Dzogchen master who established Vajrayana Buddhism in Tibet. The teachings of this lineage were first translated into Tibetan during the reign of King Trisong Deutsen during the eighth century.

OM ĀḤ HŪṂ. The three seed syllables that symbolize the body, speech, and mind of an enlightened being, such as a buddha.

Padmasambhava. The great tantric guru and Dzogchen master who established Vajrayana Buddhism in Tibet, where he is known as the second buddha (Tib. *sangye nyipa*).

paramita (Skt. pāramitā). A transcendental perfection often associated with the bodhisattva's practice of the six paramitas of generosity, ethical conduct, patience, joyous effort, meditative stability, and wisdom. The sixth paramita of transcendent wisdom is enlightenment itself.

Patrul Rinpoche (1808–1887). A great Nyingma master, bodhisattva, and Dzogchen practitioner who lived the life of a vagabond. He received instructions on the Longchen Nyingtik preliminaries twenty-five times from his perfect teacher Jigme Gyalwe Nyugu. His guide to the preliminary practices, *The Words of My Perfect Teacher*, is studied by all Khenpo Sherab Sangpo's students who practice the Dzogchen preliminary practices (Tib. *ngöndro*).

phowa. A Tibetan term for the practice of transferring consciousness at the time of death for oneself or for another.

pramana (Skt. pramāṇa). A Sanskrit term used for the scriptures on valid cognition or Buddhist logic.

rigpa. A Tibetan Dzogchen term for directly recognizing the view of the dharmakaya nature of mind and naturally resting in it.

Rongzom Chökyi Zangpo (1012–1088). Also known as Rongzompa, he was a great eleventh-century Nyingma master who met Atisha Dipamkara Shrijnana when he was young. He is renowned in Khenpo Sherab Sangpo's lineage for writing *The Jewel Commentary* on the *Guhyagarbha Tantra*.

samadhi (Skt. samādhi). Denotes the state of meditative absorption or concentration in which the mind is stable and unmoving—meaning it is held firmly without wavering.

sambhogakaya (Skt. saṃbhogakāya). A Sanskrit term which means the form body of a buddha who appears to bodhisattvas. The sambhogakaya is the basis for the arising of the nirmanakaya and it is adorned with the major and minor marks of a totally and completely awakened being.

samsara (Skt. saṃsāra). Cyclic existence or the cycle of rebirth that occurs under the control of the afflictions (*kleshas* [Skt. *kleśa*]) such as the three main poisons of ignorance, attachment, and aversion.

Sarnath (Skt. Sārnāth). The place where Buddha Shakyamuni gave his first teaching after his enlightenment to the first five most excellent disciples in Deer Park.

Secret Mantra Vehicle. See *Vajrayana*.

seed syllables. Mantric letters that are spoken and visualized in Vajrayana Buddhism that symbolize the body, speech, and mind of an enlightened being, such as a buddha or yidam deity.

shamatha (Skt. śamatha). The meditation on calm abiding or tranquility that may be practiced with or without an object.

Shantideva (Skt. Śāntideva, 685–763). The bodhisattva and great scholar of the Nalanda tradition of Indian Buddhism known for composing the *Bodhicharyavatara*.

Shariputra (Skt. Śāriputra). The Buddha's foremost hearer disciple (*arhat*) in wisdom who is mentioned in the *Prajnaparamitahridayasutra*, the twenty-five verses on the perfection of wisdom.

shravaka (Skt. śrāvaka). One who hears and proclaims, referring to a follower of the Hinayana who strives to attain the level of a foe destroyer (*arhat*).

shunyata (Skt. śūnyatā). Emptiness or the lack of inherent existence of all phenomena as taught by Buddha Shakyamuni and further elaborated upon by Nagarjuna and Chandrakirti.

siddhis. A Sanskrit term for the spiritual accomplishments that great adepts, such as mahasiddhas, attain through their spiritual practice. The supreme or uncommon siddhi is the attainment of buddhahood. See also *eight ordinary siddhis*.

stupa (Skt. stūpa). A monument that symbolizes the enlightened mind of the buddhas built to enshrine the relics of great Buddhist masters or to commemorate great events in the life of Buddha Shakyamuni.

sutra (Skt. sūtra). "Spoken discourse" or "teaching"; the entire teachings of the Buddha can be characterized as either sutra or tantra. Sutras may have been spoken by the Buddha, through his blessing, or by his mandate, indicating that the Buddha instructed his followers to compile the teachings that they had heard.

Sutrayana (Skt. Sūtrayāna). The causal vehicle that encompasses the teachings of the Hinayana and Mahayana that are followed to establish the factors (causes) for attaining enlightenment.

tantra. "Thread" or "continuum" that remains unbroken over time; the entire teachings of the Buddha can be characterized as either sutra or tantra. When tantra is presented in contrast to sutra, it indicates the texts of the Secret Mantra vehicle, variously referred to as Tantrayana, Vajrayana, or Mantrayana.

Tantrayana (Skt. Tantrayāna). See *Vajrayana.*

tsatsa. A Tibetan term for a small statue of a buddha or yidam deity that is made by pressing clay into a mold made of copper alloy.

Tsongkhapa Lobzang Drakpa (1357–1419). The great scholar monk who founded the Geluk school, known for his *Great Exposition of the Stages of the Path*, one of the canonical works of Tibetan Buddhist literature.

tukdam. A Tibetan term for the ability of great meditators to remain absorbed in luminosity at the moment of death. They may remain in this state for many days with their physical body showing no signs of decay.

Vairochana (Skt. Vairocana). The central buddha of the buddha family whose seven-point meditation posture is emulated as a support in attaining enlightenment.

Vajrakilaya (Skt. Vajrakīlaya). A wrathful yidam deity whose nature embodies the enlightened activity of all the buddhas that is practiced to remove obstacles.

Vajrasattva. A peaceful yidam deity whose nature embodies the hundred buddha families that is practiced to purify all karmic misdeeds.

Vajrayana (Skt. Vajrayāna). The Secret Mantra vehicle of skillful means that teaches a view free from confusion and is rich in methods without difficulties for those with sharp faculties.

Vajrayogini (Skt. Vajrayoginī). A semi-wrathful yidam deity whose nature embodies the enlightened energy and wisdom of all the buddhas that is practiced to generate wisdom and accomplish enlightened activity.

Vinaya. One of the three collections of Buddhist scriptures that is concerned primarily with monastic discipline.

vipashyana (Skt. vipaśyanā). Clear seeing or insight meditation that helps practitioners to develop perfect discernment—the ability to look at phenomena in a very direct and clear way.

yidam deity. A tutelary deity, buddha, or bodhisattva chosen by a tantric practitioner to support their practice. Guru yoga is a type of deity yoga in which the practitioner meditates on their root guru as the union of all of the buddhas. Practicing deity or guru yoga facilitates the recognition of the nature of mind (*rigpa*).

yogin / yogini (Skt. yogīn / yoginī). A male or female practitioner of the union (yoga) with the natural state, which is the nature of mind (*rigpa*) in the Dzogchen Nyingma lineage.

ABOUT THE AUTHOR

Khenpo Sherab Sangpo trained in Tibet with many renowned Dzogchen masters, including Khenchen Padma Tsewang and Khenchen Jigme Phuntsok, earning two degrees in Buddhist philosophy and practice from Pukang and Larung Gar's monastic universities. His innate abilities and extensive training allowed him to master the Buddhist teachings, both in terms of theoretical knowledge and experiential realization. He travels the world teaching Buddhism and is the spiritual director of Bodhicitta Sangha | Heart of Enlightenment Institute (www.bodhicittasangha.org) in Minneapolis, Minnesota, where he has taught and lived since 2006.